C

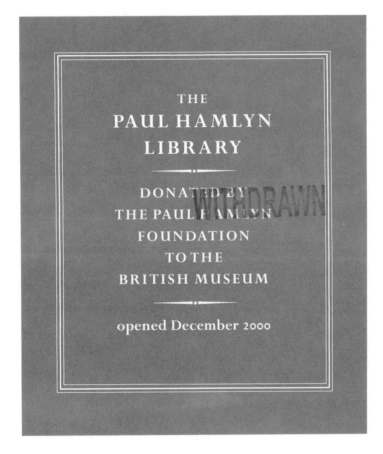

NATIVE AMERICANS AND CHRISTIANITY

Montagnais

Algonkian

Ojibwa

Crow

Dakota (Sioux)

Huron

Modoc

Northern Cheyenne

Teton (Sioux)

Iroquois

Mahican

Massachuset

Klamath

Shoshone

Comanche

Wampanoag

Narragansett

Montauk

Northern Paiute

Pawnee

Delaware

Arapaho

Southern Paiute

Ute

Southern Cheyenne

Shawnee

Powhatan

Salinas
Chumash

Osage

Cherokee

Navajo
Hopi

Kiowa

Upper Creek

Pueblo

Apache

Choctaw
Chickasaw

Lower Creek

Seminole

Arawak

Carib

Totonac

Aztec

Eskimo

Aleut

NATIVE AMERICANS AND CHRISTIANITY

Steve Klots

Frank W. Porter III
General Editor

CHELSEA HOUSE PUBLISHERS
Philadelphia

277. 008. 997 KLO

On the cover: A bilingual English-Dakota service book from The Book of Common Prayer, beaded in 1934 by Mrs. Black Fox, an Oglala of the Pine Ridge Reservation. Courtesy of the South Dakota Art Museum.

Frontispiece: The original territories of Native American tribes before contact with Europeans.

Chelsea House Publishers
Editorial Director   Richard Rennert
Production Manager   Pamela Loos
Art Director   Sara Davis
Picture Editor   Judy Hasday

Staff for **NATIVE AMERICANS AND CHRISTIANITY**
Senior Editor   Jane Shumate
Editorial Assistant   Kristine Brennan
Designer   Alison Burnside
Picture Researcher   Sandy Jones

First Printing
1 3 5 7 9 8 6 4 2

Library of Congress Cataloging-in-Publication Data

Klots, Steve.
     Native Americans and Christianity / Steve Klots.
          p. cm.—(Indians of North America)
     Includes bibliographical references and index.
     Summary: Examines the history of efforts to convert the Indians of North America to Christianity and the resulting impact on the beliefs of these native peoples.
          ISBN 0-7910-4553-6
              0-7910-4463-7 (pbk.)
     1. Indians of North America—Missions—History—Juvenile literature. 2. Indians of North America—Religion—Juvenile literature. [1. Indians of North America—Religion. 2. Indians of North America—Missions. 3. Christianity—North America—History.] I. Title. II. Series: Indians of North America (Chelsea House Publishers)
E98.M6K46 1996
277'.0089'97—dc21   96-44647
                                                                         CIP
                                                                         AC

CONTENTS

INDIANS OF NORTH AMERICA

CHELSEA HOUSE PUBLISHERS

INDIANS OF NORTH AMERICA: CONFLICT AND SURVIVAL

Frank W. Porter III

The Indians survived our open intention of wiping them out, and since the tide turned they have even weathered our good intentions toward them, which can be much more deadly.

John Steinbeck
America and Americans

When Europeans first reached the North American continent, they found hundreds of tribes occupying a vast and rich country. The newcomers quickly recognized the wealth of natural resources. They were not, however, so quick or willing to recognize the spiritual, cultural, and intellectual riches of the people they called Indians.

The Indians of North America examines the problems that develop when people with different cultures come together. For American Indians, the consequences of their interaction with non-Indian people have been both productive and tragic. The Europeans believed they had "discovered" a "New World," but their religious bigotry, cultural bias, and materialistic world view kept them from appreciating and understanding the people who lived in it. All too often they attempted to change the way of life of the indigenous people. The Spanish conquistadores wanted the Indians as a source of labor. The Christian missionaries, many of whom were English, viewed them as potential converts. French traders and trappers used the Indians as a means to obtain pelts. As Francis Parkman, the 19th-century historian, stated, "Spanish civilization crushed the Indian; English civilization scorned and neglected him; French civilization embraced and cherished him."

Nearly 500 years later, many people think of American Indians as curious vestiges of a distant past, waging a futile war to survive in a Space Age society. Even today, our understanding of the history and culture of American Indians is too often derived from unsympathetic, culturally biased, and inaccurate reports. The American Indian, described and portrayed in thousands of movies, television programs, books, articles, and government studies, has either been raised to the status of the "noble savage" or disparaged as the "wild Indian" who resisted the westward expansion of the American frontier.

7

Where in this popular view are the real Indians, the human beings and communities whose ancestors can be traced back to ice-age hunters? Where are the creative and indomitable people whose sophisticated technologies used the natural resources to ensure their survival, whose military skill might even have prevented European settlement of North America if not for devastating epidemics and the disruption of the ecology? Where are the men and women who are today diligently struggling to assert their legal rights and express once again the value of their heritage?

The various Indian tribes of North America, like people everywhere, have a history that includes population expansion, adaptation to a range of regional environments, trade across wide networks, internal strife, and warfare. This was the reality. Europeans justified their conquests, however, by creating a mythical image of the New World and its native people. In this myth, the New World was a virgin land, waiting for the Europeans. The arrival of Christopher Columbus ended a timeless primitiveness for the original inhabitants.

Also part of this myth was the debate over the origins of the American Indians. Fantastic and diverse answers were proposed by the early explorers, missionaries, and settlers. Some thought that the Indians were descended from the Ten Lost Tribes of Israel, others that they were descended from inhabitants of the lost continent of Atlantis. One writer suggested that the Indians had reached North America in another Noah's ark.

A later myth, perpetrated by many historians, focused on the relentless persecution during the past five centuries until only a scattering of these "primitive" people remained to be herded onto reservations. This view fails to chronicle the overt and covert ways in which the Indians successfully coped with the intruders.

All of these myths presented one-sided interpretations that ignored the complexity of European and American events and policies. All left serious questions unanswered. What were the origins of the American Indians? Where did they come from? How and when did they get to the New World? What was their life—their culture—really like?

In the late 1800s, anthropologists and archaeologists in the Smithsonian Institution's newly created Bureau of American Ethnology in Washington, D. C., began to study scientifically the history and culture of the Indians of North America. They were motivated by an honest belief that the Indians were on the verge of extinction and that along with them would vanish their languages, religious beliefs, technology, myths, and legends. These men and women went out to visit, study, and record data from as many Indian communities as possible before this information was forever lost.

By this time there was a new myth in the national consciousness. American Indians existed as figures in the American past. They had performed a historical mission. They had challenged white settlers who trekked across the continent. Once conquered, however, they were supposed to accept graciously the way of life of their conquerors.

The reality again was different. American Indians resisted both actively and passively. They refused to lose their unique identity, to be assimilated into white society. Many whites viewed the Indians not only as members of a conquered nation but also as "inferior" and "unequal." The rights of the Indians could be expanded, contracted, or modified as the conquerors saw fit. In every generation, white society asked itself what to do with the American Indians. Their answers have resulted in the twists and turns of federal Indian policy.

There were two general approaches. One way was to raise the Indians to a "higher level" by "civilizing" them. Zealous missionaries considered it their Christian duty to elevate the Indian through conversion and scanty education. The other approach was to ignore the Indians until they disappeared under pressure from the ever-expanding white society. The myth of the "vanishing Indian" gave stronger support to the latter option, helping to justify the taking of the Indians' land.

Prior to the end of the 18th century, there was no national policy on Indians simply because the American nation had not yet come into existence. American Indians similarly did not possess a political or social unity with which to confront the various Europeans. They were not homogeneous. Rather, they were loosely formed bands and tribes, speaking nearly 300 languages and thousands of dialects. The collective identity felt by Indians today is a result of their common experiences of defeat and/or mistreatment at the hands of whites.

During the colonial period, the British crown did not have a coordinated policy toward the Indians of North America. Specific tribes (most notably the Iroquois and the Cherokee) became military and political pawns used by both the crown and the individual colonies. The success of the American Revolution brought no immediate change. When the United States acquired new territory from France and Mexico in the early 19th century, the federal government wanted to open this land to settlement by homesteaders. But the Indian tribes that lived on this land had signed treaties with European governments assuring their title to the land. Now the United States assumed legal responsibility for honoring these treaties.

At first, President Thomas Jefferson believed that the Louisiana Purchase contained sufficient land for both the Indians and the white population.

Within a generation, though, it became clear that the Indians would not be allowed to remain. In the 1830s the federal government began to coerce the eastern tribes to sign treaties agreeing to relinquish their ancestral land and move west of the Mississippi River. Whenever these negotiations failed, President Andrew Jackson used the military to remove the Indians. The southeastern tribes, promised food and transportation during their removal to the West, were instead forced to walk the "Trail of Tears." More than 4,000 men, women, and children died during this forced march. The "removal policy" was successful in opening the land to homesteaders, but it created enormous hardships for the Indians.

By 1871 most of the tribes in the United States had signed treaties ceding most or all of their ancestral land in exchange for reservations and welfare. The treaty terms were intended to bind both parties for all time. But in the General Allotment Act of 1887, the federal government changed its policy again. Now the goal was to make tribal members into individual landowners and farmers, encouraging their absorption into white society. This policy was advantageous to whites who were eager to acquire Indian land, but it proved disastrous for the Indians. One hundred thirty-eight million acres of reservation land were subdivided into tracts of 160, 80, or as little as 40 acres, and allotted to tribe members on an individual basis. Land owned in this way was said to have "trust status" and could not be sold. But the surplus land—all Indian land not allotted to individuals— was opened (for sale) to white settlers. Ultimately, more than 90 million acres of land were taken from the Indians by legal and illegal means.

The resulting loss of land was a catastrophe for the Indians. It was necessary to make it illegal for Indians to sell their land to non-Indians. The Indian Reorganization Act of 1934 officially ended the allotment period. Tribes that voted to accept the provisions of this act were reorganized, and an effort was made to purchase land within preexisting reservations to restore an adequate land base.

Ten years later, in 1944, federal Indian policy again shifted. Now the federal government wanted to get out of the "Indian business." In 1953 an act of Congress named specific tribes whose trust status was to be ended "at the earliest possible time." This new law enabled the United States to end unilaterally, whether the Indians wished it or not, the special status that protected the land in Indian tribal reservations. In the 1950s federal Indian policy was to transfer federal responsibility and jurisdiction to state governments, encourage the physical relocation of Indian peoples from reservations to urban areas, and hasten the termination, or extinction, of tribes.

Between 1954 and 1962 Congress passed specific laws authorizing the termination of more than 100 tribal groups. The stated purpose of the termination policy was to ensure the full and complete integration of Indians into American society. However, there is a less benign way to interpret this legislation. Even as termination was being discussed in Congress, 133 separate bills were introduced to permit the transfer of trust land ownership from Indians to non-Indians.

With the Johnson administration in the 1960s the federal government began to reject termination. In the 1970s yet another Indian policy emerged. Known as "self-determination," it favored keeping the protective role of the federal government while increasing tribal participation in, and control of, important areas of local government. In 1983 President Reagan, in a policy statement on Indian affairs, restated the unique "government to government" relationship of the United States with the Indians. However, federal programs since then have moved toward transferring Indian affairs to individual states, which have long desired to gain control of Indian land and resources.

As long as American Indians retain power, land, and resources that are coveted by the states and the federal government, there will continue to be a "clash of cultures," and the issues will be contested in the courts, Congress, the White House, and even in the international human rights community. To give all Americans a greater comprehension of the issues and conflicts involving American Indians today is a major goal of this series. These issues are not easily understood, nor can these conflicts be readily resolved. The study of North American Indian history and culture is a necessary and important step toward that comprehension. All Americans must learn the history of the relations between the Indians and the federal government, recognize the unique legal status of the Indians, and understand the heritage and cultures of the Indians of North America.

The meeting between Motecuhzoma and Cortés, which took place in the spring of 1519 in Tenochtitlán, is depicted here by an Aztec artist. Cortés is flanked by his interpreter and mistress, Marina.

TWO WORLDS COLLIDING

In 1519, when the Spanish explorer Hernando Cortés sailed along Mexico's southeastern coast, news of this disturbing occurrence traveled inland to the powerful emperor of the Aztec people, Motecuhzoma. Both men no doubt knew that the arrival of Cortés was profoundly significant, but while the Spaniard eyed Mexico's lush coastline with the acquisitiveness and fervor of his Christianizing mission, the Aztec emperor, observing the steady approach of a force and type of man never before seen, must have felt a deep foreboding.

Both Motecuhzoma and Cortés belonged to civilizations that were convinced of their might and their gods. Motecuhzoma held sway over a vast kingdom of Aztec and non-Aztec nations from the capital city, Tenochtitlán, built on an island in the middle of a lake in the lush Valley of Mexico. As an empire with some 15 million subjects, the Aztecs knew no rivals, and as overlords, they demanded tribute from the peoples they had subjugated. They had built splendid temples and palaces; they studied astrology; they produced superb crafts of stone, feathers, fine cloth, turquoise, and gold; and they recorded their poetry and history in picture writing.

The Aztecs had a complex, hierarchical social system and a religion involving the worship of many gods, each one associated with some aspect of the physical or abstract universe. Tlaloc, for example, was the major fertility god, associated with rain and thunder. Huitzilopochtli was a god of war and the sun. A crucial—but, to Europeans, shocking—element of the Aztecs' religious life was their practice of human sacrifice. This they did primarily because they believed they were responsible for maintaining the universe. The sun god, for example, traveled from east to west each day. To make the journey he needed the nourishment of sacrificial human blood.

In the Aztec pantheon there was one god who hated human sacrifice. This was Quetzalcoatl, the god of maize, metalwork, and fine arts, who was depicted sometimes as a feathered serpent but occasionally as a man with a fair complexion and a flowing beard—very different in appearance from the Aztecs. Having feuded with other gods, according to Aztec mythology, Quetzalcoatl had sailed east across the ocean, vowing to return in triumph. The year predicted for his reappearance was the year One Reed—or, in European terms, A.D. 1519. This belief thus created a chink in the Aztec armor of confidence. If the fair-haired, bearded man at the helm of this great ship from the east was Quetzalcoatl returning to reclaim Mexico, then the Aztecs as mortals could not stop him.

The Spaniard, on the other hand, had no notion that he would appear as a conquering Aztec god. But what Cortés arrived with amounted to almost the same thing: a determination to claim Mexico and its riches for Spain, and a mission to convert its people to Christianity. It had been only a short time since the Genoese explorer Christopher Columbus, sailing under the standard of the Spanish monarchs Ferdinand and Isabella, had declared that he had discovered for Europe a new world lying across the Atlantic Ocean. For rulers and adventurers, this "new world" offered material riches; for the Catholic Church, it offered a wealth of souls to be won for Christ. Catholics, like virtually all Christians, hold the belief that they must spread their faith. Thus the Spanish had determined to conquer the continent for Christ and King—and they would not hesitate to advance their Christian faith with the sword.

The Spanish had settled first on islands such as Hispaniola (now the Dominican Republic and Haiti), where the native Arawak Indians innocently welcomed the strange-looking newcomers as gods. The Spanish, forcing Christianity upon the Arawaks, also exploited them as free laborers in gold mines and on plantations. Those who refused this arrangement were tortured or killed. Many others died when infected with European diseases like smallpox, to which the Arawaks had no natural immunity. This vulnerability was shared by all peoples of the "new world."

The Spanish also quickly subjugated Cuba, despite native efforts to resist. They then turned to the North American continent itself. On April 21, 1519, Cortés and a small fleet of Spanish ships sailed into a fine natural harbor near the island of Ulua on Mexico's southeastern coast. It was Holy Thursday, the day on which Christians each year commemorate Jesus' Last Supper with his disciples before his crucifixion. Cortés watched with great interest as a band of Aztecs boarded a large canoe and paddled out to the Spanish fleet.

In Mexico Cortés saw his future, for he had heard from the other Indians he had encountered of a vast empire that

The Aztecs perform a sacrifice to Huitzilopochtli, the sun god. They believed that he needed the blood of human hearts to fuel his daily journey from east to west.

glittered with gold in the highlands of central Mexico. Cortés was a man of great contradictions: often scrupulous and conniving, with a thirst for power and wealth, he was also deeply religious, praying and hearing Mass, the primary service of worship in the Catholic Church, every day. Like almost all Christians, Cortés believed that it was his responsibility to spread the Gospel, or good news, of God in Jesus Christ. Cortés thus arrived in Mexico not only as a conqueror but as one of the first Christian missionaries.

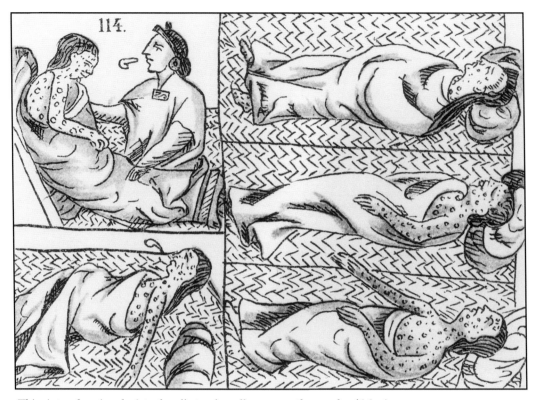

This Aztec drawing depicts the effects of smallpox upon the people of Mexico.

The Aztecs who rowed out to Cortés's fleet were welcomed and allowed to board. They had been sent as ambassadors from Motecuhzoma and carried gifts and the attire of the god Quetzalcoatl for Cortés: a sleeveless jacket, a turquoise mosaic serpent mask, greenstone earplugs and necklace, obsidian sandals, and a mirror for his back. Once aboard Cortés's ship, they insisted on dressing the Spaniard in the god's array. Cortés allowed this and then responded by firing a cannon, a novel and unnerving experience for the royal ambassadors.

Cortés went ashore on Good Friday, the day on which Christians commemorate the crucifixion of Christ. Two days later, Easter Sunday, a group of Aztecs looked on in astonishment as Cortés and his followers prostrated themselves before a rudely fashioned cross as the expedition's priest, Father Bartolomé de Olmedo, celebrated the Easter Mass. After advising Cortés to stay away from the capital city, Tenochtitlán, Motecuhzoma's ambassadors departed to report to their emperor.

While Motecuhzoma pondered whether the Spaniards were humans or avenging gods, Cortés spent several months on the coast plotting the military conquest of Tenochtitlán. The Spaniards finally marched inland, alternately fighting and gathering local peoples as they went. Cortés met enemies of Motecuhzoma—including the powerful Tlaxcalan—and convinced them to join him in his move on Tenochtitlán. During the inland march, Motecuhzoma's messengers arrived repeatedly, trying to stop the Spaniards' approach with gifts, sorcery, or blockades. But Cortés would not be discouraged or sidetracked, and in early November the Aztec and Spanish leaders finally met face to face.

Motecuhzoma had decided to welcome the Spaniards and their allies into the city and treat them as guests. Even as guests, though, Cortés and his men kept firmly in mind their goal of conquering the Aztecs and converting them to Christianity. On a tour of the city and to the top of the great temple, Cortés shocked the watching Aztecs when he ordered his troops to throw the figures representing gods down the temple steps. Soon after, Cortés took Motecuhzoma himself captive in his own city. The emperor had probably concluded by then that, avenging god or not, Cortés and his men would be triumphant.

Nevertheless, Cortés's first attempt to overtake Tenochtitlán failed, although in the fighting Motecuhzoma was killed. Cortés and his men were forced to flee the city with their Tlaxcalan allies and wait nearly six months before attacking again. In this time, however, the Spanish had been able—involuntarily—to accomplish what armed combat had failed to do: they had brought with them from Europe the deadly disease smallpox, to which the Aztecs, like the Arawak, had no immunity. Motecuhzoma's successor soon died of the disease, and it spread throughout the city.

Cortés returned in April for his next attempt to conquer Tenochtitlán. After fighting the Aztecs in the streets, the Spaniards finally withdrew, deciding instead to blockade the city and starve its inhabitants. When, after a month and a half, the Aztecs were finally weakened, the Spaniards again attacked. This time, after two and a half years in Mexico, they defeated the Aztecs. With the final submission of Tenochtitlán, Cortés claimed New Spain, as he called it, for King Charles V, and the military conquest of Mexico was complete.

While the two great armies had fought each other on the battlefields, the real conflict was between two civilizations, European and Indian (as the peoples of the Americas mistakenly came to be called, the name drawn from Columbus's presumption that he had reached the Indies). When the siege ended, the Spaniards not only had conquered a great city but also were about to change an entire culture. For the Indians, losing this war meant more than changing rulers and shifting tribute duties. The new lords of the land ruled in a way that was different from that of any Indian conquerors before them. The

Spaniards brought with them new ideas, goals, laws, and material goods that were to transform the lives of all the Mexican Indians.

The first change occurred almost as soon as the Spaniards reached Mexico: the Indian population began to decline, the result not only of warfare but also of smallpox. By 1570—only 50 years after the Spaniards arrived—the Indian population was probably one-third to one-half its preconquest size.

The daily lives of the Mexican Indians also changed dramatically. The Spaniards had brought from Europe animals that the Indians had never seen, such as horses, goats, and chickens. The Spanish also introduced new patterns of work: large gold and silver mines were established, and the Indians were compelled to work in these mines under difficult conditions. Cortés also introduced a system of work called the *encomienda* system: he gave each of his soldiers a large piece of land and made each soldier, now called an *encomendero*, responsible for the Indians who lived on it. The encomenderos were expected to ensure the well-being of their Indians and to instruct them in the Christian faith. In practice, however, most Indians became little more than slaves.

One of the most profound changes wrought by the Spanish conquerors was the spread of the Catholic faith throughout the new empire. Soon after the conquest, Catholic friars arrived in Mexico and established schools in their monasteries. Mexican children attended these schools. They learned to read, write, do

mathematics, sing, and play musical instruments. The friars' primary goal, though, was to stamp out native deities and replace them with the Christian God.

Although some tribes resisted all Spanish attempts to convert them to Christianity, the spiritual conquest of Mexico occurred with remarkable speed. In a very short time, Aztec practices that Cortés and his compatriots had found abhorrent—polygamy and human sacrifice especially—came to an end; the Spaniards also forbade the ancient tradition of eating peyote, a small, fleshy cactus with hallucinogenic properties that the Aztecs regarded as spiritual and that they consumed in special ceremonies. Soon many Mexican natives were regularly attending Mass and seeking baptism for their children.

One important reason for this openness to Christianity was the initial popularity of the friars themselves, who were often the only defenders of Indian rights against the forced labor of the encomienda system. In particular, Bartolomé de Las Casas, a Dominican friar, worked hard to reform the system and indicted the cruelty of the encomenderos and conquistadores. Despite his efforts, though, in some areas up to 90 percent of the Mexican natives died from disease and overwork.

There were other reasons that so many Indians seemed to accept Christianity. First of all, the traditional deities had been unable to stop the Spanish conquest; because the Indians were told

Spaniards destroy an Aztec religious figure under the direction of a Catholic friar. Those Indians who continued to worship their own gods had to do so secretly.

that the Christian God had triumphed over their own gods, he should be heeded. Second, most Indians, subject to the new encomienda system, learned quickly that any attempt to worship their old gods met with imprisonment and beatings. Third, there were many superficial similarities between Catholicism and Mexican religious beliefs, so the Indians quickly grasped the forms if not the doctrine of Christianity. For instance, although the friars dismissed the pagan religious images as "false idols," the new images of Mary and the saints that they placed in every Catholic church and chapel did not seem so different from the figures representing Indian gods. Fourth, the missionaries preached to the Indians in their native languages and introduced them to colorful processions marking major Christian feasts, which appealed to the Indian community.

Finally, and perhaps most significantly, the Aztec religion had been distinguished by its open character: when the Aztecs conquered another people, they added that nation's gods to their own pantheon. Thus the Aztecs were used to accepting and worshipping new gods. Upon hearing of the Christian God and his son, Jesus Christ, the

chalchicueyca

Aztecs were willing to be baptized and add the new deity to their pantheon.

As a result, in the first decade after the conquest, Spanish priests often conducted mass baptisms as entire towns converted to Christianity. The spiritual conquest of Mexico thus seemed to be proceeding quickly. But soon it became clear to the missionaries that this "conversion" was not as thorough as it appeared. It seemed instead that Christianity in Mexico was being Indianized as much as the Indians were being Christianized. This was not what the friars had intended.

For the Spanish missionaries, either one accepted Christ, rejecting all other gods as false, or one rejected Christ, thereby risking the wrath of God and Spain. The Mexican Indians, however, found they could fit this new faith and their traditional views together. They did not stop thinking as Indians, and some of their old faith crept into their adopted Christianity.

This tendency became clearest in

The Spanish encomiendo system meant that most native peoples of Mexico became little more than slaves.

the Mexican devotion to saints. In traditional Catholicism, saints are persons whose exceptional faith in this life has won them a special place in heaven, where they intercede with Christ before God on humanity's behalf. Saints are venerated for the miracles and acts of sacrifice they performed in this life, and they are petitioned for guidance and protection. For the Mexican Indians, it made sense to interpret saints as new gods in their pantheon. After their conversion, the Mexican Indians petitioned the saints as fervently as they had once petitioned their gods, especially at the small neighborhood chapels dedicated to individual saints.

The most important devotional cult within Mexican Indian Catholicism—typical of how the Indians overlaid Catholic belief upon their own—grew up around Our Lady of Guadalupe. In 1531, according to tradition, a recently converted Indian named Juan Diego saw a vision of the Virgin Mary on a hill called Tepeyac, northwest of Mexico

City (the new name for Tenochtitlán). Tepeyac also happened to be the site of a temple dedicated to Tonantzin, the goddess of motherhood in the preconquest religion. The Virgin instructed Diego to tell the bishop to build a church on the site. A few days later, Juan Diego again saw the Virgin, who this time ordered him to pick some flowers and present them to the bishop. When he did so, the flowers fell from his cloak, revealing a painted image of the Virgin that had miraculously appeared beneath them.

The bishop evidently consented to build a shrine dedicated to the Virgin at Tepeyac, for by 1533 a small church was located on the hill. Soon, various miracles were being attributed to Our Lady, as the Indians called her, and people from all over Mexico were flocking to her shrine—just as their ancestors had traveled to Tepeyac to pay homage to Tonantzin—and singing songs in her honor in Nahuatl, the primary Aztec language. For the Indians of Mexico, the Virgin's appearance at Tepeyac and the later miracles at her shrine were proof that Our Lady of Guadalupe had taken them under her protection.

Although in this way many Mexican Indians creatively adopted Christianity, others resisted. The Popolaca people and a branch of the Totonac living at Sierra de Puebla, for example, refused to go to Mass and still worshipped figures of their gods, often right alongside the images of Christian saints, well into the 20th century. Others hid their children to keep them from being baptized; an entire Indian town was discovered in 1803 to be secretly worshipping its ancient gods in a network of caves; and a parish priest found a figure of an Aztec god hidden behind an image of Jesus to which his parishioners regularly prayed.

In addition to these more secretive forms of resistance, some tribes rebelled against the missionaries aggressively. In 1541, for instance, an alliance of tribes led by the Cascanes people rebelled against Spanish authority in a conflict known as the Mixton War. In recruiting other Indians to their cause, the Cascanes spoke in decidedly anti-Christian terms:

> We are the messengers of Tecoroli [a traditional god]. Accompanied by his ancestors, whom he has revived, he is coming to seek you. . . . Those who believe in him and renounce the teachings of the friars and follow him will never die, but will become young again and have several wives. . . . Whoever takes only one wife will be killed. Then Tecoroli will come to Guadalajara, Jalisco, Michoacán, Mexico City, and Guatemala, wherever there are Christians from Spain, and slaughter them all.

Upon joining the rebellion, Christian Indians recanted their faith and symbolically cleansed their foreheads to undo the effects of baptism. But eventually this revolt was crushed, and the spiritual conquest of Mexico continued.

For Indians like the Cascanes, the

Christian faith was inherently linked with their oppressors and was to be violently resisted. For other Mexican Indians, like the Popolaca people, a less active form of resistance was the path to take. And among the Mexican Indians who did convert to Christianity, the faith many practiced was very different from that of the Spanish missionaries. Yet it may indeed have helped them to make sense of the rapidly changing world that had been thrust upon them with the arrival of the Spanish; on the other hand, it may have encouraged acquiescence instead of understanding.

Cortés would be followed by other explorers and missionaries from Spain, England, France, and Russia, who, like him, would see their futures in the continent now called America. They would arrive on both shores and would ultimately penetrate to the heart of the vast continent, encountering hundreds of tribes who had lived there for centuries. Although each tribe had its own distinctive culture, many shared traits that made them unlike Europeans: most did not believe in individual ownership of land, and most believed not in a single God but in many spiritual powers. To European settlers, these non-European characteristics made the Indians "primitive"; this view justified the Europeans'

Dominican friar Bartolomé de Las Casas was an outspoken critic of Spain's system of forced labor and wrote a treatise condemning it. He consequently earned the trust of many Mexicans.

determination to conquer and convert the Indians. In many ways the case of Mexico prefigured what would take place on the rest of the continent, as two worlds rich with their own convictions and desires collided.

The official seal of the Massachusetts Bay Colony portrays the Puritans' conception of their mission: a half-naked Indian pleads, "Come over and help us."

"COME OVER AND HELP US"

In contrast to the Spanish, the English were slow to arrive in North America. Along with the Dutch, they were the first Protestant Christians to land on the Atlantic Coast. They came in order to explore, colonize, and profit from the New World; some also came in search of religious freedom. But whether they settled as Anglicans in Virginia or as Puritans in Massachusetts, they soon also determined to convert and "civilize" the Indians they encountered—which in their minds meant the same thing.

In an area that would later be named New England, the Pilgrims at Plymouth in 1620 united themselves in the Mayflower Compact "for the Glory of God, and the Advancement of the Christian faith." In 1629 the Massachusetts Bay Colony received a royal charter from King Charles I, which proclaimed that "the principall Ende of this Plantation" was to "wynn and incite the Natives of [the] Country, to the Knowledge and obedience of the onlie true God and Savior of Mankinde, and the Christian Faith." Shortly thereafter, the Puritans who had received the charter adopted a seal for their company and colony. It featured a practically naked Indian from whose mouth issued the plaintive cry, "Come over and help us."

The seal hardly reflected the feelings of the Native Americans who inhabited the region, primarily the Wampanoag. At the beginning of the 17th century, more than 20,000 Wampanoag—an Algonkian tribe— inhabited the southeastern portion of present-day Massachusetts, the islands off its shores, and the eastern part of Rhode Island. Their territory contained forests of oak, maple, and pine, as well as rivers, streams, and wetlands. When the Pilgrims met them in 1620, the Wampanoag were competent farmers, fishers, hunters, and gatherers. All these occupations provided them with a generous and varied supply of food.

The Wampanoag had an established system of government and religion. They believed that everything that existed—deers, bears, rocks, trees—had its own special spirit; that all things lived in relation to one another; that humans must thank the spirits of other beings for providing them with the means to live. The Wampanoag also thanked the creator, whom they called *Kiehtan*, and they had religious leaders called *powwaws* who tended to their spiritual needs.

The concept of spirit power, the life force that ties together the natural and supernatural worlds, was fundamental to all Native American religions. Tapping into this power through prayers, songs, dances, and ceremonies, practitioners of Native American religions believed they could heal the sick, ensure prosperity, and protect people from harm. Native American myths and legends helped pass on cultural values and taught important moral lessons. Traditional ceremonies marked the different stages of a person's life, providing social support, introducing the person to new responsibilities and roles, and obtaining spiritual protection for the individual. Other ceremonies brought together entire communities to celebrate and affirm a common identity. And certain rituals expressed respect for the natural world and all its inhabitants. Most Native American tribes, including the Wampanoag, understood their nat-

ural environment and knew they had a role in maintaining its harmonies.

The Wampanoag therefore had no notion of needing the help of the Pilgrims and Puritans. In fact, the opposite may be more true. The Wampanoag shared their thanksgiving harvests with the Pilgrims in the 1620s; they introduced the English to corn, squash, and beans, thereby ensuring their survival in the new land; and they taught the English how to cope with the harsh winter.

But while the Massachusetts Bay Colony seal did not reflect the Indians' feelings, it spoke volumes about the Puritans' own view of their mission. They saw themselves as an integral part of God's plan of salvation for humanity: they thought that the Indians needed the Puritans to come over and help them because, lacking the light of Christ, they could not help themselves. Despite their rhetoric, however, the Puritans did not at first make much effort either to convert or to "civilize" their neighbors.

In the spring of 1642, Thomas Mayhew, Jr., the 21-year-old son of a successful merchant from the Massachusetts Bay Colony village of Watertown, sailed from Boston Harbor with several families to the island of Martha's Vineyard, off the southern coast of Cape Cod. Together with his father, the younger Mayhew hoped to establish what would amount to a fiefdom independent of the authorities in Massachusetts Bay and Plymouth Colony.

Mayhew was uncertain what sort of

The Wampanoag fished rivers and the ocean year round, using devices that ranged from spears to weirs—fencelike structures built across water flows.

life awaited him on Martha's Vineyard. According to Europeans who had explored the area, the island was perfect for settlement: its surrounding waters teemed with fish, unspoiled shellfish beds lined its shores, its lush green meadows proved the island's worth as farmland, and its rich forests could provide timber for housing and wood for cooking and heating. Nonetheless, moving to an island apart from any other English settlement was risky. But Mayhew was certain of one thing: before reaping any of the island's bounty, he would have to establish friendly relations with the Wampanoag living there.

Unlike some English colonists in America, the Mayhews did not see this new land as empty and untouched. Evidently sincere in his Puritanism and well intentioned toward the Indians,

Mayhew, upon landing at Great Harbor, negotiated the purchase of a tract of land from a Wampanoag *sachem*, or chief, named Towantquatick. Mayhew then apportioned the land to the English settlers for their individual farms, and quickly they began to re-create on Martha's Vineyard the village life of England, with tidy farms hacked out of the wilderness, a cluster of houses on the shore, and a church at its center. Mayhew himself was ordained as the village's first pastor.

Although Mayhew admired individual Wampanoag for their bravery and strength of character, like most English colonists he disdained Native Americans and attributed their alleged backwardness to "their Worship of False gods and Devils." The Wampanoag were therefore doomed to misery in this life and the next, he believed—unless he could enlighten them to the truths of Christianity.

After the initial contact between Towantquatick and Mayhew, the Wampanoag evidently kept a watchful distance from the small band of English settlers. There was, however, one Wampanoag named Hiacoomes who was curious about these newcomers. Described by Mayhew as "a Man of sober, thoughtful, and ingenuous Spirit," Hiacoomes was neither a sachem nor a powwaw but a person of little importance among the Wampanoag; in fact, some described him as "unpromising" and slow in speaking. But for whatever reason, he began visiting the English and soon became a regular visitor to the Mayhew home each Sunday night. In 1643, after a period of thought and study, Hiacoomes professed the Christian faith and was baptized by Mayhew, becoming the first Christian Indian in New England.

In adhering to Christianity, which the other Wampanoag perceived strictly as the whites' religion, Hiacoomes had chosen a difficult path. His fellow tribesmen predicted doom for him and for his family, because he had forsaken the tribal deities and shunned the powwaws, who were believed to have supernatural powers over life and death. After a time, however, the Wampanoag began to wonder at the change in Hiacoomes. Before his conversion, he had seemed slow and insignificant, but now he could speak authoritatively on many subjects. Furthermore, in 1646, he was one of a few Indians not to suffer from a plague that swept across Martha's Vineyard. Some Wampanoag began to believe that Hiacoomes had stumbled across something great, and a number of them joined him in worshipping the "white man's God." Most significantly, after hearing Hiacoomes preach, Towantquatick invited Mayhew to instruct his village in Christianity.

With Hiacoomes at his side, Mayhew preached regularly in the Indian villages, and on occasion Hiacoomes took his turn in the pulpit. For Mayhew, their success was evidence of the power of the Word of God stirring in the hearts of the Wampanoag. He had been careful to treat the tribe fairly in all matters, especially land transactions, and had done his best to lift the tribe up from what he perceived to be their misery and depravity, without trying to force English ways and English religion on them. His fairness and genuine concern for their welfare made the Wampanoag receptive to his preaching.

Another important element of the Mayhews' missionary activity was how gradually it proceeded. Mayhew and his father did not insist that potential converts abandon their traditional gods and beliefs at once; unlike the Spanish in Mexico, they did not force the Indians not to worship their traditional pantheon. The Mayhews also focused first on religious conversion and only second on cultural change. Although Thomas Mayhew never admitted finding any redeeming qualities in Indian civilization, he never forced English culture and Christianity on his Wampanoag neighbors or exploited them for their land or wealth, either.

In 1652, the Christian Indians of Martha's Vineyard asked Mayhew for his assistance in organizing a separate Christian Indian community. Five years later, they established their own church. And in 1670—by which time there were about 3,000 Christian Indians living on the islands—Hiacoomes was ordained its pastor, making him one of the first Christian Indian ministers in North America.

In 1657 the younger Mayhew was lost at sea on a return trip to England. His death was mourned by both English and Christian Wampanoag, who memorialized with stone markers the place where he had last preached to them, and the work he had started was continued by his father and his descendants. Mayhew's benevolence and success, however, were hardly typical of his New England contemporaries. Not very far from Martha's Vineyard, for instance, a Puritan minister named John Eliot, with the support of the Massachusetts Bay General Court, was attempting to bring Christianity to the colony's Indians—members of Massachuset, Nipmuck, and Narragansett tribes—by

a very different method.

In 1646, Eliot, who was the minister of the church in Roxbury, outside Boston, preached to a gathering of Indians in their native language at a place called Dorchester Mill. This first attempt, however, did not go well. "They gave no heed unto it, but were weary, and rather despised what I said," he wrote. A few months later, Eliot tried again with more success at a riverside village called Nonantum. Soon thereafter, the colony's General Court enacted a law dictating that "no person within the jurisdiction, whether Christian or pagan, shall wittingly and willingly presume to blaspheme [God's] holy name." The penalty for breaking this law would be death. Furthermore, the Court established a system of fines for observing "pagan" practices within its jurisdiction.

After this legislation, there were no repeats of the disaster at Dorchester Mills. With a captive audience, Eliot preached successfully at the Indian villages surrounding Boston. In particular, the Massachuset Indians—whom European-introduced diseases had devastated and whose culture was therefore weakened—were receptive to his message.

In 1649, the English Parliament established the Society for the Propagation of the Gospel in New England, an organization soon known as the New England Company. As the first Protestant missionary organization, the New England Company provided Eliot with funds for evangelizing the Indians of

"They gave no heed unto it, but were weary, and rather despised what I said," is how John Eliot described his first attempt to preach to the Indians of Massachusetts. Native religious practices were soon outlawed in the colony.

New England and especially Massachusetts. In sharp contrast to Mayhew, Eliot, with the legal backing of the colony and the financial support of the New England Company, soon mandated that all "praying Indians" move into Christian Indian towns—thereby separating all Christian Indians from their traditional cultures. The first of these towns was established at Natick in 1651.

Eliot hoped to win the souls of the Indians through education. Thus, each "praying town" included a schoolhouse. More importantly, in 1661 he published the Indian Bible, *Mamusse Wunneetapunatamwe Up-Biblium God,* which he had translated with the help of a Massachuset Indian named Job Nesuton and printed with the help of James Printer, a Nipmuck Indian from the praying town of Hassanamesitt. It was the first Bible published in North America in any language. By 1674, there were 14 praying towns with a total of at least 4,000 Indian inhabitants.

But in 1675 Eliot's missionary work came to an abrupt halt. As more and more English settlers had arrived in the region, increasing amounts of land had been taken for farms and towns. The

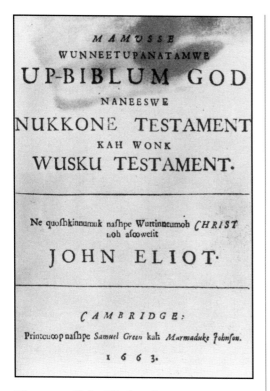

The cover of John Eliot's Indian Bible. The first published in the Americas in any language, the Bible was printed in 1661 with the help of members of the Nipmuck and Massachuset tribes.

newcomers encroached on the Indians' seasonal fishing and hunting grounds and sometimes took over cleared farming land. Relations between Indians and colonists became strained as the Indians found settlers living in their traditional fall and winter camping areas. Finally, after repeated encroachments on his territory and authority by the Plymouth colonists, a Wampanoag sachem named Metacom (called King Philip by the English), rose up in revolt and burned several towns. Soon almost all of New England was ablaze with the conflict that the colonists recorded as King Philip's War.

Some Indians who had converted to Christianity, or praying Indians, provided valuable allies and scouts for the English in this conflict. On the other hand, many praying Indians found themselves endangered by both sides in King Philip's War—they were looked on as traitors by traditional Indians, but simply as Indians by whites. Indeed, several praying towns, mostly Nipmuck, "apostatized," or renounced their new religion, and were among Metacom's first allies. In contrast, the Wampanoag of Martha's Vineyard, whom Mayhew had never forced to accept Christianity or move into separate villages, remained peaceful throughout the war, despite their close tribal kinship with Metacom.

Ultimately, the initial Indian response to Christianity in the English colonies was slow and mixed. The Narragansett, for instance, were embittered by King Philip's War and continued to reject the white man's God for several generations; the Nipmuck converted to Christianity under duress but quickly resumed their traditional ways when the chance arose; and the Massachuset tribes turned to Christianity only when their traditional beliefs and practices failed to shield them from the disastrous effects of English migration. Only the Wampanoag of Martha's Vineyard seemed to welcome Christianity, but even they must have sensed the impending threat of English domination.

Throughout the colonies, the result was the same. Missionary success depended on the extent of European-Indian contact and the destruction of Indian society. "Come over and help us," the Puritan had imagined the woeful Indian as saying, but for the most part, this slogan was rhetoric used to justify a European conquest of America that was hardly "Christian" or "civilized."

In the early 1700s, new missionary efforts were underway throughout the colonies. A group called the Society for the Propagation of the Gospel in Foreign Parts (SPG), founded in England, had evangelical, benevolent, and political intentions. While still intending to spread the Gospel among the Indians, the SPG also hoped to lessen the ill effects of English settlement upon the Native American population—namely vice, such as alcoholism, and disease. This group also did not always attempt to "civilize" the Indians while evangelizing them. According to one SPG missionary in 1767, "I have observed that those Inds. who have the least intercourse with us, have the most integrity, & possess the best Moral Qualities."

At the same time that the SPG began its efforts, another new missionary enterprise was underway in the South by members of the Moravian Church. The Moravians were unusual as missionaries in colonial America, as they believed that all persons, no matter how different in appearance, were made in the image of God and capable of hearing the Gospel. Unlike the SPG, the Moravians came not as emissaries of the English crown and culture—being themselves mostly German—but as witnesses to the Gospel. They formed close communities and reached out to the Indian villages in the surrounding countryside.

But despite these new movements, colonial leaders in New England continued to insist that Indians be brought into the fold of Christian "civilization," primarily through education. Many tribes in fact welcomed the missionaries, whom they hoped would help them keep their shrinking lands. A few even converted to Christianity. Yet many tribes in turn-of-the-century New England held fast to their traditional beliefs, especially in Connecticut and Rhode Island. A member of the Mohegan tribe, for example, said that his people "could not see that men were ever the better for being Christians, for the English that were Christian would cheat the Indians of their land and otherwise wrong them."

There were many reasons that Native American groups would not adopt the religion of the white colonists. Aside from the hostilities engendered by land conflicts, the introduction of diseases, and the simple irrelevance of Christianity to many Indians' way of life, Christianity as preached by missionaries was simply too austere. The Christianity of New England was in many ways a religion of the head, not the heart.

Around 1740, however, a movement of spiritual renewal known as the Great

Awakening swept through the churches of New England and the mid-Atlantic colonies and radically challenged the character of colonial Christianity. Traveling ministers like James Davenport of Southold, Long Island, whipped the populace into a spiritual frenzy using an emotional style of preaching. These so-called New Light preachers attacked the rigorous intellectualism of 18th-century Puritanism. Instead they spoke of a more individual religious experience that involved trances, revelations, and spontaneous oratory that came from the heart and not the mind. Perhaps most important, they attacked the Old Light ministers who based their religious authority on formal education instead of on a spiritual calling.

The Great Awakening made Christianity more accessible to the Indians along the eastern seaboard. Many Indians could relate to the notion of a religious leader whose power derived from a spiritual calling, because their traditional powwaws and other religious men and women had principally based their authority on such a calling. In addition, the New Light stress on revelations, visions, and spontaneous oratory struck a familiar chord with the Indian tribes, who had always valued visions and oratory and who still found "book learning" an alien concept.

During the Great Awakening, many tribes that had held on to their traditional beliefs converted to Christianity. For instance, the majority of the Narragansett were converted after Davenport preached near Stonington, Connecticut,

in 1743. Other tribes such as the Wampanoag, portions of which had long espoused Christianity, joined the New Light movement and established Separate or Separate Baptist churches.

The Great Awakening ultimately produced a surge of Christian Indian leaders who were concerned for the spiritual and physical well-being of their people; perhaps the most remarkable of these was a Mohegan named Samson Occom. Born in 1723, Occom was a member of a respected Mohegan family and a descendant of their great sachem Uncas. He attended various Indian missionary schools while growing up, mainly because the missionaries often awarded their students food and blankets. He remembered the Great Awakening reaching his village at Uncas Hill:

> When I was 16 years of age, we heard a Strange Rumor among the English, that there were Extraordinary Ministers Preaching from Place to Place and a Strange Concern among the White People. . . . But we Saw nothing of these things, till Some Time in the Summer, when some Ministers began to visit us and Preach the Word of God; and Common People also Came frequently, and exhorted as to the things of God.

Their exhortations did not fall on deaf ears. "I was one that was Impresst with the things we had heard" wrote Occom. Convinced of the truth of Christianity, Occom applied himself to learning "English letters," using a primer and

Metacom—known to the English as King Philip—fought the colonists' encroachments upon Indian land in a revolt that inflamed most of New England. Even many "praying Indians" renounced their new faith and joined the Wampanoag chief.

seeking help from his English neighbor, but attending no school. In 1743, when he was 19, he began taking lessons from the Reverend Eleazar Wheelock, a moderate New Light minister at Lebanon, Connecticut. "When I got up there, he received me With kindness and Compassion and instead of Staying a Fortnight or 3 Weeks, I spent 4 years with him."

In 1749, Occom was called to serve as schoolmaster to the Montauk, an Algonkian tribe living on the tip of Long Island. Ten years later, he was ordained a Presbyterian minister, preaching as often to English as to Indian congregations. In the meantime, he helped his tribe's sachems fight their land disputes with the Connecticut General Assembly. Most important, he

Ridley & Blood Sc.

Rev. Samson Occom,

Indian Preacher.

Pub. by Williams & Smith Stationers Court 10 Oct. 1808.

The fiery oratory of the Great Awakening captivated a young Mohegan named Samson Occom. Under the tutelage of Connecticut minister Eleazar Wheelock, Occom became the first Native American to publish a work in English.

became respected even in the English community as an eloquent speaker and preacher. In 1772, his *Sermon Preached at the Execution of Moses Paul, an Indian* became the first work published in English by an Indian author. The sermon, detailing the confessions of a Mohegan convicted of committing murder while under the influence of alcohol, was so popular that its publishers reissued it at least 19 times.

After the Great Awakening subsided, Wheelock, inspired by Occom's example, opened Moor's Indian Charity School near his church in Lebanon, Connecticut. The object of the school was to separate young Indians from their tribes and instruct them in the basics of white culture: boys learned Latin, Greek, Hebrew, and "husbandry"; girls learned reading, writing, and "housewifery."

Soon, however, the American Revolution brought an end to most work by the churches among the Indians throughout the English colonies. After more than a century of missionary activity, many of the Indian tribes of what would soon become the United States were more or less Christian, especially those tribes that had lived close to European settlements for decades. In New England, some tribes had established their own independent churches. A new tribe of Christian Indians was even formed and—feeling distinct from white Christians and wanting to retain an element of their own culture— bought their own tract of land; Occom joined them in 1785 and said of their new home, "We Named our Town . . . Brothertown . . . and Concluded to live in Peace, and in Friendship."

Samuel de Champlain, founder of "New France" (present-day Quebec), invited Jesuit missionaries to work among the Huron and Iroquoian peoples. The Jesuits believed that any means justified their goal: the salvation of Indian souls for the greater glory of God.

3

BLACK
ROBES

As English Protestants took their message to the Native Americans of the eastern seaboard, well-meaning French Catholics extended their mission to the Indians along the icy banks of the St. Lawrence River in present-day Canada. Whereas the English were colonizing in the East with the intention of settling permanently, the French at first were more interested in trading with the Native Americans—exchanging the woven cloths, metal implements, and weapons of European culture for the furs of animals that the Indians were so skilled at trapping.

Fur trader Samuel de Champlain established the first French trading post, Quebec, in 1608, and he quickly befriended the Montagnais and other Algonkian tribes, as well as the Huron. Although the Huron spoke an Iroquoian language, along with the Montagnais they were hostile to the Iroquois, who lived south of the St. Lawrence River and had established a

league that included the Mohawk, Oneida, Onondaga, Cayuga, and Seneca. In 1609, Champlain and his men helped a Huron war party defeat a band of Iroquois. This skirmish sealed the French alliance with their Huron and Algonkian neighbors but earned the newcomers the hatred of the Iroquois, which would ultimately limit the scope of the French Jesuit mission to North America.

In 1625, Champlain invited a group of Jesuit priests to minister to the small colony of Quebec. Founded in 1540 by Saint Ignatius of Loyola, the Jesuits' goal was the salvation of all men and women through the Catholic faith. Trained as a soldier, Loyola understood this goal in terms of spiritual warfare—against the devil, sin, paganism, and all heretics, or dissenters from church belief. For Loyola, the end justified the means, if the means resulted in the salvation of a soul in the Catholic faith for the greater glory of God. Jesuit missionaries were thus prepared to endure any hardship and use any means to spread the faith. On the American continent, this would mean trying to gather Native Americans into self-sufficient communities ruled by the Jesuits—through the destruction of the Indians' traditional culture and beliefs.

The Montagnais, however, were satisfied with their own civilization and theology. They had adjusted ingeniously to their surroundings: in winter, they made inland camps to hunt moose, elk, and sometimes caribou. In summer, they settled along the present-day Gulf of St. Lawrence, fishing the bountiful ocean, as well as the lakes and rivers. Like many Native Americans, they held religious beliefs involving animal spirits. They believed that every living thing had spiritual power and that the balance among beings must be maintained; animal spirits permitted some of their number to be caught for food, for example, and the Montagnais must give thanks for this to ensure continued survival. They observed specific rituals to show their gratitude, such as always keeping the bones of game animals together and disposing of them with reverence. Thus, rather than seeking a single being's salvation from sin to attain eternal life, the Montagnais and other Algonkian tribes of the St. Lawrence River region sought to remain in harmony with nature during this life.

The Jesuit priests invited by Champlain were at first interested in creating seminaries for Native American boys. Other than a few orphans, however, the Jesuits—who were called "black robes" by the Indians because of their clerical garb—had very few people to instruct in the fundamentals of their faith. Thus, when Father Paul Le Jeune, the Superior of the Residence at Quebec, was invited in 1633 to join a band of Montagnais on their winter hunt, he jumped at the opportunity. He realized, however, that the Indians were more interested in his food supply than his teachings.

For five months, Le Jeune roamed the wilderness with the Montagnais, enduring hunger, cold, and the ridicule of his companions. One of them was a man with the French name of Pierre, who had been educated and baptized in the early years of the colony but had then reverted to his native religion. Pierre and his brother, a Montagnais shaman, repeatedly antagonized Le Jeune. At one point, Le Jeune was encouraged when the brother, whom the Jesuit referred to as the "sorcerer," offered to help translate Christian doctrine into the Montagnais language. With the shaman's help Le Jeune began preaching one night to the rest of the Montagnais, who burst out laughing at him; the "sorcerer" had tricked him into explaining Christianity in exceedingly foul terms. On another occasion, after several days of bad hunting, the Montagnais told Le Jeune they would pray to his God for success. The eager priest made the Indians kneel before a crucifix and pray for Christ's guidance. The hunting went well that day. When Le Jeune suggested at mealtime that they give thanks to God, however, the Indi-

A Huron couple and their child. Before French contact, the tribe called themselves the Wendat, *or "the people"; the French renamed them the* Huron, *or "the savages."*

ans scoffed.

When Le Jeune returned to Quebec that spring, he was convinced that the Algonkian people would never accept the Christian faith as long as they maintained their lifestyle. He became an advocate of small, permanent Indian villages that depended on the French for their existence. Once again, Christianization was seen as "civilization."

Indeed, by this time, the traditional life of the Montagnais had begun to erode. The busy fur trade had caused a drop in the population of game animals around Quebec and had actually tethered the Montagnais to the French settlement as they grew increasingly dependent on European goods. There was also the horror of European diseases—smallpox, influenza, and measles—to which the Montagnais, like all Native Americans, had no

The frontispiece of Recollet priest Gabriel Theodat de Sagard's book, Long Journey to the Country of the Huron. *In 1632, the French government forbade the Recollets, a Catholic order, from visiting North America. Sagard hoped that by publishing the story of his 1623 visit, he would persuade the government to reconsider the ban.*

natural immunity. When traditional Montagnais shamans proved powerless against epidemics, some Indians turned in desperation to the black robes' God for help.

The result was limited Jesuit success in Christianizing the Algonkian tribes around Quebec. Although the missionaries failed in their pursuit of seminary education for Indian boys, who could not tolerate the confinement of a European-style upbringing, the priests had better results with adults. The mission town of Sillery, near Quebec, for example, started with two Montagnais families in the 1630s; between 1638 and 1640, the church at Sillery recorded 118 baptisms. But this could occur only after the breakdown of traditional life.

The Jesuits also wanted to establish churches among the Huron. In fact, after Father Le Jeune returned from his ill-fated winter hunt with the Montagnais in 1633, three of his Jesuit brothers traveled west on the St. Lawrence and Ottawa rivers to the Huron village of Ihontaria. At their friend Champlain's urging, the Huron welcomed the missionaries, one of whom—Jean de Brebeuf—had visited two years earlier and earned the tribe's respect. But although the Hurons were fascinated by the accoutrements of French civilization brought by the missionaries—woven fabrics and clocks, for instance—they had no interest in the Christian faith. "It is good for the French, but we are another people, with different customs," said one Huron to de Brebeuf.

Their traditional territory, to the south and west of the Montagnais, allowed the Huron—who called themselves the Wendat—to live a more sedentary life. They settled in farming villages, moving only every decade or so as they depleted the soil of nutrients.

Corn was their staple crop; they traded any surplus with the northern Algonkian tribes in exchange for beaver pelts and moose skins. The corn crop was the responsibility of Huron women, and although men grew no food crops, they did grow tobacco for religious and ceremonial pipes. Women supplemented their families' diet by gathering wild grapes, acorns, and onions; the men hunted whitetail deer and bear.

As the Huron depended so heavily on corn for sustenance, they worshipped corn spirits in addition to animal spirits. They held dances and feasts to entreat the spirits' help during famine or to thank them in times of abundance. They also believed in dream interpretation as a route to spiritual well-being. The *ononharoia* ("turning the brain upside down") ceremony was the Huron people's best tonic against spiritual affliction. Participants ran from house to house, asking neighbors through riddles to give them whatever it was they had dreamed about the previous night. A woman who dreamed of weeding her garden, for instance, would hint through riddles and pantomime until someone offered her some land to cultivate. Although the first Jesuits to visit the Huron saw this ritual as primitive and childish, the ononharoia actually reveals great psychological sophistication: the Huron recognized the destructive potential of repressed desires and so devised a symbolic way to reveal and fulfill them.

While the ononharoia was a preventive ceremony against spiritual ailments, Huron religion also sought to cure physical illnesses. Certain people were believed by the community to have supernatural healing powers. Huron spirituality emphasized preventing and treating disease, so curers were especially important people.

The arrival of de Brebeuf and the Jesuits in Ihontaria ushered in something that rendered even the curers powerless, though. In all likelihood they introduced smallpox to the Huron, who died in droves. The Jesuits traveled from family to family, ministering to the sick and exhorting the Indians to accept baptism before dying. Despite the Jesuits' urging, most Huron were not interested in receiving baptism, even if it did mean a secure place in heaven. "Heaven is a good place for Frenchmen," said one Huron, "but I wish to be among Indians, for the French will give me nothing to eat when I get there."

Smallpox so devastated Ihontaria that the Jesuits fled, moving their mission to the village of Teanaustaye for a short time, and finally to the shore of Lake Huron in 1640. Called Sainte-Marie-des-Hurons, the mission served primarily as a fortified refuge from Iroquois attacks. The hardships that the Jesuits willingly endured and their kindness in the midst of the tribe's sufferings moved many Indians to accept Catholicism at least nominally by the latter half of the 17th century. Other Huron, however, accused the black robes of casting an evil spell on the tribe.

Although many Huron were now

baptized, they did not abandon all of their customary tribal practices or their enmities—especially toward the Iroquois. Because the Iroquois deeply resented France's trade alliance with their enemies, and the spread of French Catholicism was evidence of that hated alliance, Huron Christians were prime targets for capture, torture, or enslavement. The Iroquois seldom spared adult male captives. Their custom called for ritual torture of prisoners by burning or dismemberment. In Iroquois culture, captives who bore this torture bravely died with honor.

Much to the horror of the Jesuit missionaries, the ostensibly Christian Huron were no different from the Iroquois in this respect. In the rare event that the Hurons were victorious in battle with the Iroquois, they exacted swift revenge; de Brebeuf saw Iroquois captives ridiculed, mutilated, and burned at the stake. When he once spoke of the need to forgive one's enemies, some Huron responded by throwing the severed limb of an Iroquois warrior into his church. After de Brebeuf baptized a dying Iroquois, one Huron asked him, "Why did you baptize that Iroquois? He will get to Heaven before us, and, when he sees us coming, he will drive us out."

In 1646, after a brief pause in the fighting between the two groups, the Iroquois renewed their hostilities against the French and their Huron and Algonkian allies. Already weakened by disease and famine, the Huron and certain Algonkian tribes were nearly destroyed during the ensuing years:

hundreds were killed, and many more (especially women and children) were forced to join the victorious tribe, where they were usually adopted into families. Father de Brebeuf himself was captured and tortured to death in 1649. One remnant of the Huron fled southwest, while another merged with a small related tribe called the Tionnontates and migrated to a French settlement called Ancienne Lorette, across the St. Lawrence from Quebec. There, the surviving Huron and the Tionnontates, as well as the devastated Algonkian tribes, sought the protective custody of the French.

The Huron and the Algonkian tribes remained at Ancienne Lorette for 24 years. Protected from Iroquois attacks, their population recovered and grew, necessitating a final move to a Jesuit mission eight miles north of Quebec in 1697. They named their permanent home Jeune Lorette.

The Jesuits had come to New France nearly 75 years earlier for the greater glory of God, promising eternal life in Christ. In the Jesuits' estimation, God had been served; at long last, in Jeune Lorette the Jesuits had their settled Christian Indian village. Jesuit missionary Paul Ragueneau wrote,

I came up this river only thirteen years ago. I found it bordered with Algonquian tribes, who knew no God, and in their infidelity thought themselves gods on earth; for they had all that they desired—abundance of fish and game, and a prosperous trade with allied

A detail from a 1657 French map of New France, showing a converted Huron couple praying.

nations: besides, they were the terror of their enemies. But since they have embraced the Faith and adored the cross of Christ, He has given them a heavy share in this cross, and made them a prey to misery, torture, and a cruel death. In a word, they are a people swept from the face of the earth. Our only consolation is, that, as they died Christians, they have a part in the inheritance of the true children of God.

Satisfied that the end had justified the means in converting the Huron and Algonkian tribes, the Jesuits turned their attention to those Indians whom they believed to be most firmly in Satan's grasp: the Iroquois. As prisoners of war, some Jesuits had already attempted to evangelize the Iroquois. As he traveled through Huron territory in 1642, missionary Isaac Jogues was captured by Iroquois warriors. After mangling his hands to prevent him from baptizing a dying Huron chief, his captors carried Jogues to the Mohawk village of Tionnontoge. Believing that a martyr was doubly blessed by God, the missionary was not afraid to die for his faith, so went around the village ministering to its Christian Huron prisoners and attempting to convert their Iroquois captors. He then escaped to the Dutch settlement at Fort Orange.

Jogues returned to the Iroquois in 1646, during a brief truce between the tribes, to bring the sacraments to their Christian Huron captives. Unfortunately for him, however, the four years between his visits were marked by epidemics and crop failure. The Iroquois, deciding that Jogues was the cause of their troubles, killed him by splitting his skull—making him a doubly blessed Christian martyr in the end.

The efforts of men like Jogues—and the Iroquois' recognition that friendship

The 1649 execution of Father Jean de Brebeuf by his Iroquois captors. In this illustration, de Brebeuf stoically bears ritual cutting and scalding—earning Christian martyrdom and the respect of the Iroquois.

with the Jesuits might open trade with France to them—paved the way for a Jesuit mission in the Onondaga village of Gannentaha. Founded in 1655 and called Sainte Marie, the mission survived for three years until attacks by non-Christian Iroquois forced its evacuation. Many Iroquois resisted conversion because an Indian accepting Christianity ran the risk of being ostracized by his or her family. This was a grievous price to pay in a culture that highly prized the ties of kinship. But one young Iroquois woman, a Mohawk, would transcend these circumstances and influence countless Catholic Indians.

In April of 1656, a baby girl was born to a Mohawk chieftain and his wife, an Algonkian who had been baptized, raised by a French farmer, and then kidnapped by the Mohawk at the age of 12. The couple named the girl Ioragode ("Sunshine"), because she had been born at dawn. Although her mother quietly practiced her faith without the ministrations of a priest, Ioragode was reared in the traditions of her father. She was orphaned at an early age, however, when smallpox ravaged her village, killing her parents and leaving her with a pockmarked face and damaged eyes. Following Mohawk custom, she was adopted by her uncle, Iowerano, and her two aunts.

Iowerano took good care of his adopted daughter. Because her poor vision forced her to navigate their longhouse—a type of wooden house in which the Iroquois lived—by sense of touch, Iowerano renamed her Tekakwitha ("She Pushes with Her Hands"). Iowerano was a Mohawk traditionalist, refusing to drink the alcohol that Dutch settlers traded to the tribe and avoiding the Jesuits and their message. When peace was made with the French in 1667, however, several Jesuit missionaries came to the village and soon after constructed a chapel.

Missionary Isaac Jogues preaches to Mohawks. Believing that he was to blame for the epidemic that followed his arrival, they later killed him.

According to the traditional Jesuit account of her life, Tekakwitha was a spiritually inquisitive child who prayed to know Rawanniio, the Great Spirit. Upon seeing some Mahican prisoners tortured to death, she is supposed to have wept and said, "It is wrong. Rawanniio loves all human beings. He does not want us to find pleasure in torturing and killing our captive enemies." In 1675, she defied Iowerano and told one of the Jesuits, Father Jacques de Lamberville, of her desire to become a Catholic. After several months of catechism, she was baptized on April 5, 1676—Easter Day—and was given the Christian name Kateri, the Mohawk version of Catherine.

Kateri Tekakwitha became a devoted worshipper at the village's little chapel. Although Iowerano, recognizing her determination, did nothing to stop her, she suffered daily ridicule from other villagers and verbal abuse from her aunts. Finally, during the visit of a distant relative who was a Christian from the St. Francis mission, Kateri realized that she would have to leave home to practice her faith in peace. While her uncle was away on a trading expedition, she fled.

In October of 1677, Kateri arrived at

the mission after several weeks of travel on foot and by canoe. She came highly recommended to the Jesuit priest there; Father de Lamberville had written a note that said, "Kateri Tekakwitha now comes to join your community. Granting her your spiritual guidance and direction you will soon realize what a jewel we have sent you. Her soul is very close to the Lord."

Kateri's new home bore some resemblance to the praying villages of New England. On the advice of their Jesuit priests, the village chiefs prohibited drinking, quarreling, and traditional religious practices. Although all visitors were welcomed hospitably, whites and non-Christian Indians were not allowed to live in the village. Mass was said three times a day in the village chapel. The language of the church was Latin, but the Jesuit fathers also translated several hymns and prayers into the Iroquois language, which the Indians sang both in the chapel and at their chores.

For the first time in her life, Kateri could practice her faith without fear. When not doing her chores, she devoted herself to prayer and self-sacrifice. On Christmas Day of her first year in the village, Kateri was allowed to make her First Communion. She insisted on wearing plain clothing without any jewelry, wampum pearls, or glass beads in order to emulate the humble ways of Christ.

Kateri became known to the villagers as their "angel in the flesh." When most of the village left for the annual winter hunt, Kateri stayed behind to devote herself to praying,

fasting, and caring for the frail elderly. On a trip to Montreal, she met a small group of nuns and realized she had long yearned to live as a nun—never marrying but dedicating her life to the love of Jesus. Kateri spent her days in penance for sins that she believed she had committed before her baptism.

After months of fasting and serving others in God's name, Kateri became weak and emaciated. In the spring of 1680, feverish and nearly unconscious, she received Communion and Last Rites. After kissing a crucifix and whispering a prayer, Kateri slipped into unconsciousness and died. According to the Jesuit account of her death, a miraculous change came over her body at the instant life left it: her face became radiant, free of the ravages of her childhood bout with smallpox.

The story of Kateri's miraculous death spread quickly among the Catholic Indians of New France, and her grave soon became a place of pilgrimage. Iroquois and Huron Christians alike found strength in their belief that God had chosen an Indian to be an example of such innocent faith, and they prayed to Kateri for guidance and comfort. Numerous Indians reported miraculous healings and blessings after praying to Kateri Tekakwitha.

In 1760, the English conquest of Quebec curtailed the Jesuit mission to the Iroquois, and their conversion to Christianity would mostly be left to Quakers from Pennsylvania, Puritans from New England, Moravians from Germany, and Anglicans from New

New Faith and Traditional Vision

As European culture overtook the Americas, many Native Americans responded to the newcomers' promises of salvation by converting to Christianity or adopting elements of the new religion in their own rituals and beliefs. The images that follow show some of the ways that Native Americans participate in Christianity today, blending their faith and their creativity. The pictures of gifts given to the Reverend Frank M. Thorburn, a white Episcopal priest on the Standing Rock and Pine Ridge reservations from 1931 to 1952, are of particular interest. In these beautiful items, the ancient Sioux tradition of giving honor gifts intersects with contemporary Christianity in unexpected and poignant ways.

Inside and out, this beaded hymnal exemplifies the mingling of Native American tradition and 20th-century Christianity. The book contains both English and Dakota lyrics, and its cover was beaded by Amelia Iron Necklace, a Sioux woman from the Standing Rock Reservation, as a gift for Reverend Frank M. Thorburn in 1932. Mrs. Iron Necklace explained that "the front red beads with eagle are for the Dakota." The blue "1928" at the bottom of the design commemorates the year that Mrs. Iron Necklace's husband died. (color photo 1)

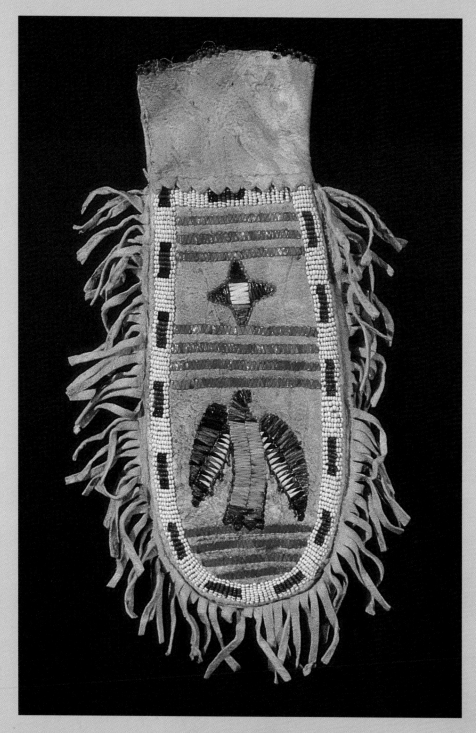

Front view of a beaded pipe sack, made in about 1940. It was a gift to Reverend Thorburn from parents hosting a Victory Dance to celebrate their son's return from World War II. Thorburn attended several such traditional dances on the Pine Ridge Reservation, where he was presented with gifts to thank him for his prayers for the safe return of young Lakota soldiers. (color photo 2)

This watch fob is probably a Sioux design, because its entire surface is covered in the blue pony beads typical of such work. When an everyday item such as this was adorned with Christian symbols, its owner was expected to wear it during all church services and ceremonies. (color photo 3)

Mayan Indians in Guatemala hold a religious procession. The two figures on the float represent Mary and Jesus Christ, but they are dressed in the colorful clothing of traditional Mayan culture. The peoples of Mexico infused the Christian teachings of the early missionaries with their own colorful pageantry. (color photo 4)

Three hundred years ago, Catholic missionaries tried to remake Native Americans in the image of white Europeans. Today, church doctrine and Indian visual traditions coexist freely, as demonstrated by the exterior of this Catholic Church in Wyoming. (color photo 5)

The interior of a Catholic church in Santa Fe, New Mexico—believed to be the oldest church in the United States—as it appears today. (color photo 6)

A worshipper kneels before the altar of a Russian Orthodox church on Kodiak Island, Alaska. Aleuts and Eskimos adopted the Orthodox faith more readily than many other Native Americans accepted Christianity—perhaps because the first Orthodox missionaries to Alaska were outspoken advocates of native rights, protesting the abuses of Russian fur traders who virtually enslaved the Indians. (color photo 7)

Kateri Tekakwitha defied Mohawk tradition and left her home to follow the Catholic faith. After her First Communion, she was a servant of God, praying, fasting, and caring for others until her death in 1680. The Vatican took a step toward declaring Kateri Tekakwitha the first Native American saint by beatifying her in 1980. (color photo 8)

Kateri Tekakwitha, "the lily of the Mohawks," was exceptional in her lifetime as an Iroquois who devoted herself to the Catholic Church despite the ridicule of her own family. Devout and self-sacrificing, she died at the age of 24 and was later beatified.

York. For the Catholic Indians of Quebec, however, nothing would alter their veneration for the young woman they remembered as "the Lily of the Mohawks."

Despite individual stories like that of Kateri Tekakwitha, European attempts to Christianize Native Americans in Quebec had a bitterly ironic twist: traders and missionaries introduced deadly diseases, encouraged dependence on commercial goods, restricted Native American movement, and then held out Christianity as a source of comfort as the Indians' way of life eroded before their eyes. Soon the native peoples of the west coast would face the same experience.

This 1790 engraving depicts the Russian settlement of fur trader Gregory Shelikov on Three Saints Harbor, Kodi-ak Island.

4

PERSUASION AND FORCE ALONG THE PACIFIC

While the fiery English preachers of the Great Awakening evangelized New England Indians, and Catholic Iroquois began praying for Kateri Tekakwitha, explorers from Russia and Spain began charting the continent's Pacific Coast. In 1728, Vitus Bering briefly explored the Alaskan coast for Russian czar Peter the Great; 13 years later, Bering returned to Alaska for a more thorough inspection and discovered an abundance of sea otters—thereby initiating the Alaskan "Fur Rush."

In a very short time, encampments of *promyshlenniki*—Russian trappers and fur traders—dotted the Alaskan coastline. These camps were neither permanent colonies nor formally affiliated with any church. Most promyshlenniki who came to Alaska intended to stay only a few years to trap sea otters, so they left their families behind in Russia. They did, however, bring their Russian Orthodox religious beliefs.

Although not official emissaries of any religion, they informally established the Orthodox Church in their new surroundings. In time, many of these promyshlenniki married native wives—Aleuts and Tlingit Indians—and raised children, whom they baptized and instructed in the Orthodox faith. Thus, these journeymen hunters in effect became missionaries.

One fur trader, Gregory Shelikov, was particularly successful and soon began negotiating with the Russian government for a monopoly over the industry. Relations between individual promyshlenniki and Alaskan natives had often been brutal, and Shelikov claimed a desire to protect the Aleuts in asking for a monopoly—although a battle resulting from his takeover of Kodiak Island killed several hundred Sugpiaq Aleuts. In petitioning for a monopoly, Shelikov asked that 10 Russian Orthodox monks be sent to Kodiak

Island. Before they came, Shelikov himself established a school whose curriculum included the rudiments of Christianity. His motives for Christianizing the native people were suspect: while he sincerely believed in the superiority of Christianity to native spirituality, Shelikov also reasoned that by baptizing the Indians, he would create a compliant labor force for his fur-trading outfit.

Shelikov had described the settlement on Kodiak Island in glowing terms, so the monks who arrived in 1794 were horrified to find the natives in virtual slavery: women were forcibly kept as mistresses, even by men who had wives in Russia; children were abused; and men were forced to hunt at gunpoint for sea otters. The monks denounced the promyshlenniki for their inhumanity, and the Aleuts welcomed the supportive presence of the monks on Kodiak Island.

The most vocal defender of the native people's rights was an Orthodox monk known simply as Hieromonk (Father) Herman. He was the spiritual leader of the Kodiak mission; his school and orphanage on Spruce Island did much to strengthen the Russian Orthodox faith among the Aleuts. Exploited by the promyshlenniki, the native Alaskans were also ravaged by the diseases that initial contact with whites inevitably brought. Hieromonk Herman gained a reputation among the people for his piety and compassion, ministering to them until his death in 1837.

Following Orthodox practices, the monks of Kodiak came as emissaries not of Russian culture and civilization but of Jesus Christ. In Orthodox belief, a culture—whether Russian or native Alaskan—has no value except as a means of conveying the Gospel. Therefore, the monks of the Kodiak mission did not share the zeal of the Jesuits or Anglicans for "civilizing" their new congregants. Aided by Osip Priannishnikov, the son of a promyshlennik and an Aleut woman, the monks dedicated themselves to learning about the native Aleut and Tlingit cultures and religions in order to find the best way to present Christianity as a preferable alternative. They looked for parallels between the native Alaskan religions and the Russian Orthodox Church. For example, the creation myth of Sedna, mother of the sea beasts so vital to life in Alaska, bears some resemblance to the Christian account of Adam and Eve: just as Eve sprang from Adam's rib, so the whales, walruses and seals came from the joints in Sedna's fingers. By emphasizing similarities, however tenuous, between the native traditions and Christianity, the monks introduced the island's natives to Jesus Christ without forcing them to refute their native beliefs.

The Russian Orthodox mission spread throughout coastal Alaska, reaching from the Tlingit Indians of the southeast to the Inuit of the Yukon delta on the Arctic coast. In time, many of the missionaries were themselves natives or the children of Russian men and native women. Such intermarriage helped spread Christianity, as did the mission-

Inuits in winter dwellings made of blocks of ice. The houses were often lined with stones, whalebone, or skins, and they were sometimes built close together with passageways between.

aries' offer to teach willing converts how to read and write. Eager to create an indigenous Alaskan Orthodox Church, the monks wanted to groom native people for the priesthood and other religious vocations. In 1807, for instance, Hieromonk Gideon took three promising native students back to Russia with him, and in 1842, Alaskan Bishop Ivan Venianimov opened an Orthodox seminary at the capital city of New Archangel (now Sitka).

One key to the success of the Rus-

sian missionaries might be found in the strict observance of ceremony that marked the native Alaskans' original faith. Father Ivan Venianimov observed in 1824 that the Aleuts were fastidious in attending confession, taking communion, and complying with fasts. These were a people who had adhered to an elaborate code of rituals and taboos—such as neatly lining up seal skulls to face a new hunting camp and never mixing the meat of land and sea animals, as a show of reverence toward the

St. Michael's Cathedral, the Russian Orthodox Church in Sitka, was built in 1834. Several years later, Father Ivan Veniamov founded a seminary in Sitka to prepare Alaskan natives to spread the Gospel to their own people.

dwellers of both realms—which may have helped them adopt the ceremonial trappings of Christianity. Venianimov also noticed, though, that the Aleut Christians had little understanding of the theology behind their new rituals.

When Russia sold its Alaskan territory to the United States in 1867, many of the promyshlenniki went back to their homeland across the Bering Sea, and Russian support for the Alaskan mission was sharply curtailed. But native missionaries remained among

their people to infuse feasts, healing ceremonies, and traditional stories with Christian elements, developing a uniquely indigenous Orthodox culture.

The introduction of Russian Orthodoxy to Alaska, although largely successful, did not come without a price. When the United States purchased Alaska, the Aleut population was approximately 2,500; before Russian contact, it had been about 15,000. While much of this destruction is attributable to the fur traders' brutality, the missionaries themselves—here as elsewhere— unwittingly killed members of their own churches by infecting them with diseases like smallpox, measles, and influenza.

At the same time that the first promyshlenniki were settling on the Alaskan coast, the Spanish far to the south were expanding into an area they called Alta California. Under the military leadership of Gaspar de Portol and the spiritual guidance of Junipero Serra, a Franciscan friar, the Spanish built their first mission and *presidio* (fortified post) in present-day California at San Diego in 1769. Within a dozen years, the coast from San Diego to San Francisco was sprinkled with missions.

According to Serra, the move into California was undertaken "by order of His Majesty . . . . for the greater honor and glory of God, and the conversion of the Infidels to our Holy Catholic faith." Since the days of Columbus and Cortés, the Christian faith had been used to justify Spanish expansion; this time, Spain's underlying motive was to prevent the Russians from moving farther down the Pacific Coast.

The California mission system was the apex of Spain's efforts to convert native peoples in North America. As early as 1540, Spanish explorers traveled northeast from Mexico in search of a mythical, bejeweled city called Quivira. This expedition ultimately failed, as did a subsequent one in 1580. Just as Cortés and his men had done in Tenochtitlán, these Spaniards spilled a trail of native blood through the Sierra Gorda and into present-day New Mexico, Arizona, and Baja California.

The main difficulty Spain encountered in trying to convert native peoples of the Southwest was the strength of their existing religions. The Pueblo Indians of New Mexico, for example, believed that their place in the natural order required them to be good-hearted and to perform complex rituals; failure to do so would upset nature's balance and induce catastrophe. It is not unlikely that the Pueblo saw the Spanish invasion as one such disaster.

The Chumash of coastal southern California also had an elaborate set of ceremonies that fit their circumstances. The sandy soil of their region made agriculture impossible, but they were expert gatherers, attuned to the life cycles of all indigenous plants, and they rounded out their diet by fishing and hunting when animals were available. According to the Chumash, everything in the natural world possessed spiritual power, so religion was part of all daily activities. They believed that they could perpetuate the fragile balance of nature by showing their reverence to nature spirits in prescribed ceremonies. The Christianity taught by the Spanish seemed irrelevant to their daily concerns.

As the Spanish reign extended into California, the church continued to rely upon coercion to convert native peoples. In the Sierra Gorda, inhabited by the Pame people, wrote one witness, "the captain of the soldiers sent a sergeant with a detachment of troops to burn all the houses of the Indians that were scattered through these sierras, so that they would then live together in the new town. . . ." In this way, the natives of Sierra Gorda were gathered into presidios, where they were simultaneously converted to Catholicism and subjugated to the authority of Spain. As in Mexico centuries before, by forcibly reshaping their subjects' lives, the missionaries hoped to render their native religions irrelevant once and for all.

Serra continued this strategy in California. In his diary, he described the "conversion" of one Indian. When two unconverted Indians approached his entourage, several converted Indians among Serra's men

> went to catch them with caution, that they should not escape them. And altho' one fled from between their hands, they caught the other. They tied him, and it was all necessary, for even bound, he defended himself that they should not bring him, and flung himself on the ground with such violence that he scraped and bruised his thighs and knees. But at last they brought him. They set him before me, and setting him on his knees, I put my hands upon his head and recited the Gospel of St. John, made the sign of the Cross upon him, and untied him. He was most frightened and very disturbed.

In this manner, scores of California natives, who came from branches of the Salinas, Chumash, and Shoshone tribes, were introduced by the Franciscans to the Christian faith. Others who came

willingly to the missions were held captive once they had converted to Catholicism and received baptism. Those who attempted to escape were hunted down and captured by the Spanish troops. When Indians rebelled against this tyranny—as they did in San Diego in 1776—they were put down even more harshly. Thus, the presidios and missions of California operated under the guise of religion to preserve Spain's military authority.

Serra himself, however, was not without compassion. He had left a promising career as a theologian in order to work for the "salvation" of the natives of Mexico and California, enduring illness, famine, and hardship along the way. He was, however, blind to the devastation wrought by the Spanish missions of California. Before the Spanish conquest, the region's natives had lived self-sufficient lives as hunters and gatherers. Contemporary Spanish witnesses speak of the natives as being well fed and healthy. In the missions, however, the Indians were forced to become farmers in order to feed the priests and military personnel. Torn from their traditional means of survival, they became helpless in times of drought—frequent in this area, which, as the Indians' way of life attested, was unsuitable for farming. The native population of California decreased dramatically.

The California missions damaged the surviving Native Americans in more subtle ways, too. The peoples between San Diego and San Francisco spoke

V. R. DEL V. P. F. JUNIPERO SERRA

The California mission system, led by Franciscan friar Junipero Serra in the 1770s, was the apex of Spain's effort to convert the native peoples of North America.

many dialects in the Salinan, Chumash, and Shoshonean language groups. Rather than learning all of these dialects, the Franciscans forced the Indians to speak Spanish at the missions. The Franciscan friars also confined unmarried men and women to separate quarters and permitted no intermingling; such restrictive European mores clashed with native customs and further fueled the Indians' rejection of Christianity.

In 1784, Serra died at San Carlos Borromeo in Carmel, where he was buried with full military and naval honors. For another 50 years, the California missions remained under Franciscan control. If anything, time only made conditions worse for the Indians. In 1799, Father Antonio de la Concepción Horra, himself a Franciscan, visited the California missions and was horrified

by what he saw: "The treatment shown to the Indians is the most cruel I have ever read in history," he wrote. "For the slightest things they receive heavy floggings, are shackled, and are put in stocks, and treated with so much cruelty that they are kept whole days without a drink of water."

By some estimates, three-fourths of the region's Indians died from famine and disease during the course of the Franciscan mission to California. Even after the missions were secularized (put under the control of a diocesan bishop, who relied on lay persons to carry out his orders) in 1834, conditions did not improve for the native tribes. The civilians who replaced the friars began to

As a group of Indians looks on, Father Serra supervises the raising of a cross to establish the mission at Santa Barbara, California.

steal and sell the missions' land and resources. Within a decade, the missions dissolved, and the Indians—some of whom had been born on the missions and knew no other life—became ordinary parishioners who were no longer supported by the church.

Thus, although they had abandoned most of their way of life and their beliefs in exchange for the new religion and new culture that swept through their regions, the Indians of California ultimately were left with almost nothing. A similar shock would be experienced by the Cherokee in the lush woodlands of the Southeast, in a conflict that would put to the test the founding principles of the newly formed United States.

Robert Lindneux's painting of the Cherokee Sequoyah. The Cherokee were quick to adopt the legal and economic systems of white culture, and they accepted mission schools so that their children would learn English. Sequoyah, however, devised a Cherokee alphabet to give his people a medium for preserving their own culture.

5

"CIVILIZATION" AND REMOVAL

When the colonies rose up against the British to wage the American Revolution, Native Americans were enlisted to take sides. Some joined the British, believing that in this way they could stop the American colonists' encroachments on their lands. When the war ended with the victory of the American colonies—soon to be called the United States—many Native Americans were considered defeated enemies.

The new government then declared that all the land east of the Mississippi River was its property. But much of this land was occupied by native tribes, so this early policy soon provoked conflict and bloodshed between American settlers and Indians. By 1789, the government, now under President George Washington, had developed a new policy: it would purchase land from Indians, rather than simply claim it. While purchasing land, the government would, like the English missionaries and colonists earlier, try to "civilize" the Native Americans. If Indians were "civilized," they could melt into mainstream American culture.

The goal was both well intentioned and racist. It was also at odds with the desires of most settlers, who simply wanted to take the land. They did not believe the Indians had any right to the land because the Indians, rather than farming individual plots, used it communally for hunting or group farming. Despite the settlers' impatience, the government began its efforts to "civilize" the Indians by convincing them to give up hunting for settled farming and to abandon their religions for Christianity.

Beginning in the 1790s, a movement known as the Second Great Awakening swept through the churches of the new country. Like its namesake 50 years earlier, the movement precipitated an outpouring of religious emotionalism and evangelical action and launched the grand era of worldwide Protestant missionary work. Steeped in millenarianism—a belief in the Second Coming of Christ that would establish the Kingdom of God on earth—evangelical Protestants felt it was their duty to spread the Gospel around the globe to prepare all persons for Christ's return—indeed, to hasten that return. As part of this, American Protestants felt a special responsibility to evangelize the "heathen" in their own land. Throughout the United States, missionaries returned to the chapels and schoolhouses that their denominations had abandoned during the Revolution.

The Second Great Awakening also instilled in many Protestants a sense that the young, idealistic Unites States had a special role in establishing the Kingdom of God. Because they feared that God would find the country wanting, some Protestants organized into the Evangelical United Front. This was a coalition of benevolent societies with objectives ranging from temperance and the abolition of slavery to the establishment of Sunday schools. These missionary societies aimed not just to win the Indians for Christ, but to transform their lives here on earth as well.

The Cherokee were one of the first tribes to encounter this new sense of Christian purpose. A tribe of Iroquoian descent, the Cherokee traditionally occupied land that included portions of present-day Tennessee, Alabama, Ken-

tucky, Georgia, Virginia, and the Carolinas. Their lifestyle, like that of many other southeastern tribes, stressed community and included both hunting and agriculture. They called themselves the "Principal People," had an extensive body of myths tying them to their land, and believed in their role in maintaining the balance of nature. Like other tribes, they had experienced steady encroachments on their land by white settlers. In 1786, they traded a large portion of it to the government in exchange for guarantees that there would be no more encroachments. Many Cherokee, however, realized that the pressure would continue, and they sought different ways to resist or adapt to the new nation.

Although the Cherokee had been in frequent contact with the English colonists of Virginia and North Carolina, only the German Moravians had established a mission settlement among them at the time of the Revolution—in western North Carolina in an area they called Wachovia. These settlers failed to convert the Cherokee to Christianity but were warmly regarded. The Cherokee called the Moravians' main settlement at Wachovia the "fort where there are good people and much bread."

In 1800, the Moravians obtained the consent of a Cherokee council to open a school at Spring Place, in present-day Georgia. The Cherokee, however, were not so much interested in learning the Christian faith as in learning English and preparing their children to lead the tribe into the future.

Over the next three decades, several

Despite the Cherokee's rapid assimilation of white culture, President Andrew Jackson ordered them and the other "Civilized Tribes" to move west of the Mississippi when he signed the 1830 Indian Removal Act.

Protestant denominations established mission schools on Cherokee land. In 1803, a Presbyterian minister named Gideon Blackburn opened a school on the Hiwassee River in Tennessee, and in 1816, Cyrus Kingsbury of the American Board of Commissioners for Foreign Missions (ABCFM) established a school near Missionary Ridge in what would become Chattanooga. In 1822, the Methodists opened a mission school and preaching circuit near Paint Rock, Alabama. In time, mission stations of all the major Protestant denominations dotted the Cherokee landscape.

At Blackburn's school, students spent the day singing hymns and studying the Scriptures, geography, arithmetic, and grammar, with little time off for play. Separated from their parents, Cherokee children learned other aspects of white American culture: boys were taught not to hunt but to farm; girls were taught not to farm but to keep

Samuel Austin Worcester, a missionary who fought for the repeal of the Indian Removal Act, was arrested for his actions by the state of Georgia and sentenced to four years' hard labor.

house. Although not interested in a missionary education for themselves, many parents insisted on it for their children, and the tribe as a whole gave a portion of its government annuities— yearly payments for land—to support the schools. Many Cherokee had decided that these changes in their culture were in their own best interest and would enable them to keep their remaining lands. Some, however, believed that to keep their lands at the expense of their culture would be a greater loss.

Beginning in 1819, when the War Department announced the establishment of a "civilization fund," these mission schools also received the support of the federal government. According to Blackburn, the missionaries would "not only rescue the rising race from savage manners, but also . . . light up beacons, by which the parents might gradually be conducted into the same field of improvement." Through these mission schools, the churches transformed

Cherokee society in a very short time.

An 1826 survey showed the tribe to be extraordinarily acculturated. There were Cherokee farms, schools, cotton mills, blacksmith shops, and ferries. Some Cherokee had become extremely wealthy, living on plantations and owning black slaves. John Ross, principal chief of the Cherokee at this time, was a notable example of such prosperity: he lived in a well-appointed two-story home, oversaw a plantation, and ran a ferry on the Coosa River in North Georgia. His friend Joseph Vann lived even more spectacularly in nearby Spring Place, eventually owning more than 100 slaves for his 300-acre plantation.

In 1827, the Cherokee adopted their own constitution and started a bilingual newspaper, the *Cherokee Phoenix*. Its first editor was the Cherokee Elias Boudinot, who had been one of the first converts to Christianity at Spring Place. Ironically, the paper was able to print in Cherokee as well as in English thanks to the invention of a written form of the Cherokee language by a man named Sequoyah. He had intended, however, not to ease his tribe's absorption into white culture but to provide a means for preserving its own culture.

Although many Cherokee, like Sequoyah, resisted the religion of white Americans, others, like Boudinot, were extraordinarily receptive to the spiritual message brought by the missionaries. While the Cherokee respected the Moravians for their honesty and hard work, the singing and preaching of Methodist and Baptist camp meetings appealed more to their religious instincts. Many Cherokee traveled with the missionaries, serving as translators and exhorters in their native language, and in 1826, the Tennessee Conference of Methodists appointed Turtle Fields, a full-blooded Cherokee, to a preaching circuit for white and Indian congregations. As a traveling preacher, Fields went from village to village, preaching wherever a crowd might gather.

Because of its willingness to adapt to white American culture, the Cherokee soon became known as one of the "Five Civilized Tribes" of the South, the other four being the Choctaw, Chickasaw, Seminole, and Creek. A large portion of the tribe had taken on all the trappings of contemporary white American culture, from Christianity to plantations to republican laws. The Cherokee nation had even, thanks to Sequoyah's invention, become the most literate nation in the world.

Despite all this, white settlers coveted the Cherokee's flourishing farms, rich forests, and gold-filled mountains. They were indignant that these "savages" could stand in the way of their own progress. Thus, in 1829, the Georgia legislature passed a bill that nullified the Cherokee constitution, asserted the state's authority over Cherokee territory, and called for the registration of all whites living on Indian land. Furthermore, in 1830, President Andrew Jackson pushed the Indian Removal Act through Congress, claiming that it was in the best interest of both Indians and whites. It demanded that all Indians move to a territory west of the Mississippi River. In particular, the legislation targeted the Five Civilized Tribes, all of which had shown remarkable adaptability to European "civilization."

Since the first days of European colonization, many Indians had been moving west—some to avoid white settlers, some just to survive, and some to escape conflicts within their own tribes. Indeed, by 1830, several hundred Cherokee had already emigrated to Indian Territory. Many Christian ministers sincerely advocated Indian emigration as the best thing for their spiritual and physical well-being.

Many missionaries, on the other hand, believed that forced, government-legislated removal was a grave injustice. To steal the Cherokee's land was the same as destroying their identity as a people. These missionaries asserted that the legislation was wrong in principle and practice and that, furthermore, it would hardly protect the tribes from the nation's continuing westward expansion. In addition, they feared that this forced removal would permanently turn the tribes against all facets of "civilization," including the Christian faith.

Jeremiah Evarts, a member of the ABCFM, spearheaded the campaign in Washington against the legislation. Using the pseudonym "William Penn," Evarts argued the case against removal in a series of widely distributed essays. His argument rested on two points: first, the right of the Cherokee to their land as established by treaty and by their existence on the land from time immemorial, and second, his conception of the United States as a nation with a Christian purpose. God had called the United States to be a beacon of Christian hope in a corrupt world, asserted Evarts, and the Indian Removal Act went against that purpose. If implemented, it would be nothing short of a national sin, incurring the wrath of God upon the nation.

Other missionaries fought not with the federal government but with that of Georgia. On July 7, 1831, the Georgia militia arrested three ABCFM and two Methodist missionaries for living in Cherokee territory without a permit from the state; all white men had been required to register with the state so that it would be easier to distinguish them from the Cherokee. These missionaries had refused to obtain the permits because they did not recognize Georgia's power over the Cherokee. The ministers were chained together and forced to walk more than 70 miles to the prison at Camp Gilmer, where they were kept in squalor. Two of them— Samuel Worcester and Elizur Butler— were later convicted of the offense and sentenced to four years' hard labor in prison.

Worcester and Butler carried their case to the Supreme Court, which on March 3, 1832, ruled that Georgia indeed had no jurisdiction over the tribe. President Jackson, however, ignored the ruling, and ultimately Congress ignored Evarts's pleas to repeal the Indian Removal Act. Treaties ceding their land were forced upon the Chero-

Robert Lindneux's 1942 painting The Trail of Tears *depicts the Cherokee's forced march from their homelands to new Indian Territory west of the Mississippi.*

kee.

In 1838, soldiers rounded up the Cherokee and forced them to march west. It was a march that the Cherokee would remember—for the loss of their homeland and the deaths of thousands from disease and starvation along the way—as the Trail of Tears.

White greed for Indian land had brought the United States to one of its darkest moments. The Five Civilized Tribes—the Cherokee in particular— learned that accepting white civilization and Christianity made them no more a part of white America than they would have been while preserving their own culture. By now, however, the transformation had been made. At the same time, some white Christians learned that advancing the faith did not necessarily mean advancing the cause of the nation—indeed, they learned that being a Christian could conflict with being an American.

As white culture moved westward throughout the 1800s, U.S. forts sprang up across the Great Plains to protect white settlers from the tribes who were angered at the encroachments on their land.

6

"DESTINED TO COVER THE EARTH"

Almost all of the large Eastern tribes and many of the small ones were ultimately compelled to move west of the Mississippi River. The Delaware, for instance, began a sojourn that took them through Canada and parts of the Great Plains until they too landed in what Congress had dubbed Indian Territory, in present-day Oklahoma. Even some tribes that had long practiced the Christian faith went west, sensing that otherwise they were faced with cultural if not numerical extinction. In this vein, small tribes such as the Brothertown Indians moved to Wisconsin.

Other tribes, however, reacted to the removal policy by explicitly rejecting the missionaries and their message. For instance, a remnant of the Seminoles withdrew into the swampy Everglades, where for decades they resisted all encroachments by white settlers, government agents, and Christian mission-

aries. The Creek Nation made the practice of Christianity a penal offense between 1845 and 1848; they associated their forced removal with the missionaries and wanted no part of assimilation or "civilization."

Those tribes that had moved to Indian Territory were, for the time being, safe from further white encroachments. Many tribes already west of the Mississippi, however, were not so fortunate, especially those on the Great Plains.

The Plains—the semiarid region stretching from present-day Colorado to Canada—were inhabited by the Lakota Sioux and other tribes, such as the Cheyenne and Crow. Ever since the introduction of horses by European settlers, these tribes' lives had revolved around the buffalo who roamed the vast land. The Lakota depended upon the buffalo for food, clothing, and shelter; mounted on horseback, they carefully tracked and hunted the migrating herds.

Like other Native American tribes, the Lakota understood the supernatural realm to be inhabited by many different kinds of spirits. All spirit beings and entities were considered *wakan*, or sacred. The most important beings were the sun, sky, and earth, and next important were the spirits of winds, the four cardinal directions, the thunderers, buffalo, and bear. A special role in the Lakota religion was given to a deity called White Buffalo Calf Woman, who is said to have brought peace and knowledge to people and to have given them a sacred pipe they could smoke to send messages to the supernatural world. White Buffalo Calf Woman also gave the Lakota the rituals that were crucial to their lives, especially vision quests and the Sun Dance.

The Sun Dance was an annual ceremony of great solemnity, often involving large groups of related tribes. The most dramatic moment was when the ceremony participants danced around a sacred pole in a construction called the Sun Dance lodge. The dancers were actually attached to the pole by means of skewers piercing the skin of their chests; they would dance until finally they could tear themselves free. In doing this, the dancers endured pain and showed bravery to increase the strength of their community. The Sun Dance united all members of the Lakota community and allowed them to express their gratitude to the spirits for the bounty of their universe.

The Lakota, like other Plains tribes, had had limited encounters with white explorers and traders for at least a century. But in 1849, gold was discovered in California, and suddenly, white fortune seekers began to pour across the Great Plains in record numbers on their way west. As these gold seekers forged routes west, they hunted the buffalo that roamed the Plains, and they left behind a trail of wagon ruts, garbage, and their own perished kin. Both the buffalo and the tribes that depended upon them were disrupted by the steady stream of migrants, and hostilities frequently broke out.

The migrants themselves were followed by settlers, who staked claims to Indian lands and then demanded that their government protect them from the justifiably angry tribes. In treaty after treaty, Indian tribes traded portions of their traditional lands for government annuities and guarantees against further land grabbings. Time and again the treaties were broken and ignored, especially when gold was discovered in these lands themselves.

With these settlers and fortune seekers came missionaries from nearly every Christian denomination—the direct result of the evangelical fervor that had defined American Christianity since the Second Great Awakening. Combined with the young republic's growing sense of nationalism, this religious zeal engendered the doctrine of Manifest Destiny, a belief that the United States had a Christian duty to expand westward, whether this meant seizing Texas and the Southwest from Mexico or dec-

Europeans first introduced horses to the people of North America, changing forever the lives of tribes like the Lakota Sioux. But missionaries and U.S. government officials later insisted that Indians abandon their hunting way of life, as depicted here by George Catlin.

imating the Indian tribes of the Great Plains. As the century progressed, racism deeply pervaded this doctrine of Manifest Destiny: from Charles Darwin's theories of evolution and natural selection, some whites derived a notion that all nonwhites, including Native Americans, were racially inferior and incapable of adapting to "civilization."

In contrast to popular sentiment, most church missionary groups were more hopeful about the future of American Indians. The churches saw their Indian mission work in this expanding American frontier as an integral part of their preparions for the coming Kingdom of God. They were concerned for the spiritual and physical well-being of the Indians, and the congregations, parishes, dioceses, and church districts of the East organized on behalf of their Indian "brothers." Although they still believed that Indian culture was savage, they also believed that Indians could adapt to Christian civilization; this belief arose from their faith that "with God nothing will be impossible." In addition, they believed that all persons,

even the Indians, were children of God.

Nonetheless, these missionaries believed that for Indians to survive, they must accept the faith that, in the missionary view, was synonymous with white civilization. Wrote Stephen Riggs, an ABCFM missionary to the Lakota,

"As tribes and nations the Indians must perish and live only as men! With this impression of God's purposes as they are being developed year after year, I would labor to prepare them to fall in with *Christian civilization* that is des-

tined to cover the earth."

As with their predecessors, Protestant missionaries to the Plains established schools to educate the Indians in Christianity and civilization. ABCFM missionaries among the Osage in Kansas, for instance, compiled *Wabashe Wageressa Pahogreh Tse: The Osage First Book,* which they used to teach their younger charges the alphabet and moral lessons from Scripture. Lured by the promise of clothing and food, students would attend a school until supplies ran out. Yet even among tribes that

An Oglala chief's painting of the Sun Dance. One of the most grave ceremonies among many plains tribes, the Sun Dance tested young men's endurance and bravery and was believed to strengthen the entire community.

had opted to use their annuities for educational purposes, attendance was sporadic. The missionaries could not understand why, for instance, a pupil would rather go on his or her tribe's annual hunt than stay at the mission, learning the alphabet and working the station's fields.

Not to be outdone by their Protestant rivals, Roman Catholic missionaries were reaching out to the tribes of the Great Plains and the West at the same time. A Jesuit priest named Pierre-Jean De Smet was probably their most famous missionary. A Belgian by birth, De Smet began working full-time as a missionary to the Indians in 1838. A gentle, courageous man, De Smet was ultimately more successful in coordinating Catholic mission efforts than in mission work itself; he was, however, often helpful in averting bloody conflict between Lakota and whites. Through the work of Jesuits like De Smet, Catholic missions soon dotted the American and Canadian West.

The Civil War brought a temporary halt to almost all missionary work in the

United States. After the war, white migration to the West resumed with even greater vigor, increasing the demand for Indian land. The white settlers' renewed westward push and the Plains tribes' strong resistance to this encroachment set off incidents of heightening violence. So too did the government's failure to deliver the annuities and food promised to those Indians who had agreed to give up their land. Tribes like the Santee Sioux of Minnesota, kin of the Lakota, had yielded land and their traditional livelihood of hunting only to find the government failing to deliver the food and supplies the tribe now depended upon. Finally they were driven to riot in their desperation. The result was that white settlers demanded even more fervently that Indians be removed or exterminated.

Some missionaries who understood the sources of tension from the Indian point of view began to clamor for a reassessment of the nation's Indian policy. This was especially the case after an incident of particular horror, the 1864 massacre of at least 400 Cheyenne—many of them women and children who were either sleeping or running for their lives—at Sand Creek by U.S. soldiers.

In 1867, Congress designated a "Peace Commission" to explore and address the reasons for continued Indian hostilities. The commission's report was a harsh indictment of predatory white behavior, especially that of the federal agents who grew rich from the fraud committed by the "Indian Ring," the bureaucracy in Washington and on the reservations that was meant to protect Indian interests but usually swindled the tribes out of their due.

The report sparked renewed concern for the Indians among the churches. "The truth is," commented one religious journal, "that there are three obstacles to the salvation of the Indian—Indian Rings—Western hostility—and the Indian's depravity, and the three ought to be met in the order we have named them." Over time, the interests of church and state merged. A Washington newspaper suggested that members of the Society of Friends, or Quakers, be called in to run the Indian agencies; in addition to their reputation for honesty, the Quakers had been well received by the Indians since the days of William Penn. Similarly, a group of concerned Christians headed by the Right Reverend Henry B. Whipple, Episcopal Bishop of Minnesota and an advocate for Indian rights, spoke in private to the newly inaugurated President Ulysses Grant of the need to reform the Bureau of Indian Affairs.

The result was informally called Grant's Peace Policy. President Grant first replaced the corrupt appointees in charge of the Indian agencies in Kansas and Nebraska with Quakers. Then he appointed an independent Board of Indian Commissioners, composed of 10 lay Christians, to oversee a fund of $2 million "to maintain peace among and with the various tribes, bands, and parties of Indians, and to promote civilization." Finally, on the advice of the Indian Commissioners, he allotted the

SITTING-BULL.
SIOUX.

E.A.BURBANK.

"Our religion seems foolish to you," Lakota Sioux Sitting Bull *once said to a mission school teacher, "but so does yours to me."*

remaining Indian agencies to an array of churches, both Protestant and Catholic. In essence, the missionaries of these churches became paid government agents.

It was a well-intentioned move, and for a time it succeeded. In the absence of fraud, better and more plentiful supplies were distributed to the tribes through the Indian agencies. The missionaries, as official representatives of church and state, continued to present Christianity as synonymous with "civilization," and they had a captive audience in the Indian tribes, now mostly confined to reservations.

But civilization meant abandoning traditional lifestyles, and, again, not all Indians were eager to adopt the settled life offered by the missionaries. Many Lakota Sioux, for example, refused to relocate to small reservations. The famous Battle of the Little Big Horn took place in 1876, when large bands of Lakota and other Plains tribes gathered for their annual hunt and Sun Dance, despite government demands that they report to a reservation. The Indians were attacked by George Custer but managed to rout his troops; later the

event was billed by horrified whites as a massacre. The prominent Lakota leader Sitting Bull, who had been at the battle and later fled to Canada, explained why he had refused to live on a reservation:

> If the Great Spirit had desired me to be a white man he would have made me so in the first place. He put in your heart certain wishes and plans, in my heart he put other and different desires. Each man is good in his sight. It is not necessary for eagles to be crows.

In contrast, when an Ojibwa named Nebuneshkung converted to Christian-

Lakota Sioux await rations. Although some plains Indians found solace in Christianity, others were simply demoralized by their new lives on reservations.

ity, he asked an Episcopal missionary to cut his hair, an act that was, for him, an obvious symbol of his new life and the sacrifice he was making in forswearing his old ways:

If the Great Spirit has so big a love for poor Indian, surely Indian ought and must give back great love. . . . Now, dear Brother, to be true to return my love to the GREAT SPIRIT, I brought this scissors, to have you cut my hair locks which I shall throw away for ever.

Other Indians, upon converting, immediately adopted western dress and became farmers. In many instances, Indian converts joined the missionaries in spreading the Gospel, but in doing so, they often showed a remarkable contempt for the traditional way of life. For instance, in 1870, Paul Mazakute became the first Lakota to be ordained as an Episcopal priest. "I grew up among [my people] sad and wretched," wrote Mazakute on his death bed, "but at last I found a blessed Faith, having which, though I am dying, I know that I am waiting for a great joy and peace." Mazakute earnestly hoped that his children, in his absence, would be reared by whites so that one of them might return to the Lakota to continue his ministry.

For many Indians, the rivalry between Protestants and Catholics was confusing. They rightly asked why they should convert to Christianity when the purveyors of the faith could not agree on what it meant to be a Christian in the first place. "Our religion seems foolish to you," said Sitting Bull to a mission schoolteacher, "but so does yours to me. The Baptists and Methodists and Presbyterians and the Catholics all have a different God. Why cannot we have one of our own?"

In the end, these denominational jealousies and the opposition of frontier whites (who had profited from the old, corrupt system) led to the demise of Grant's Peace Policy in the United States. Protestants and Catholics alike judged that it seemed rather arbitrary for a board in Washington to determine the denominational loyalties of the var-

ious tribes, and anti-Catholic organizations like the American Protective Association protested the use of any public funds to support Catholicism. H.M. Teller, Secretary of the Interior under President Chester Arthur, finally dismissed the policy.

Nonetheless, by the end of the 19th century, some members of most tribes in the United States or Canada had to some extent accepted the Christian faith, although, in more isolated areas, a few tribes (such as the Hopi) continued to resist all attempts at evangelization. The era of Grant's Peace Policy sealed the relationships that exist between certain tribes and denominations to this day—for instance, between large portions of the Sioux and the Episcopal Church, and between many tribes of the Pacific Northwest and the Methodist Church. The missionaries had set themselves to their task with the best of intentions, but in the end, had played a role in the destruction of the Indian way of life.

For a few Indians, the new faith did help to relieve their suffering. In 1886, Delaware Chief Charles Journeycake recounted how his tribe had been forcibly moved six times and deprived of their land. In Missouri, where for a time the Delaware had lived peacefully as farmers, whites had stolen their cattle and their farms. "We try to forget these things," said Journeycake. "But we would not forget that the white man brought us the blessed gospel of Christ. The Christian hope. This more than pays for all we have suffered."

Perhaps because the Mormons originally moved west to escape persecution themselves, their missions were relatively sympathetic to Indians. Mormon elder Daniel McArthur is here shown baptizing Paiute converts in Utah.

But for others, the promises of the Gospel were hollow. Deprived of their traditional way of life, they became dependent on government subsidies that were often inadequate and, in any case, demoralized them by stripping them of their self-sufficiency. For these Indians, the Christian faith as preached on the reservations was meaningless. And not a few Indians hoped for a different sort of faith: one that was clearly Indian, able to speak to their brothers and sisters who were rapidly being overwhelmed in their native land.

"When the sun died, I went up to heaven and saw God and all the people who had died a long time ago": the words of Wovoka, the Paiute prophet whose vision stirred the Ghost Dance movement of 1889. This photograph of a Ghost Dancer was taken by anthropologist James Mooney in 1893.

7

"THE DEAD ARE
ALL ALIVE AGAIN"

From the first years of European contact, some Indians, while explicitly rejecting the Christian faith as presented by European missionaries, had unconsciously absorbed Christian ideas into their tribal belief systems. For instance, in the first years of the Jesuit mission at Quebec, northern Algonkian tribes such as the Montagnais scoffed at the Christian idea of heaven and hell. They were certain that all Indians, when they died, went to the land of the dead, situated in the west at the setting sun, where they would enjoy themselves hunting, feasting, and dancing; the Algonkian had no belief in a hell where the wicked were punished for their misdeeds in this life. Heaven and hell were places a European might go, but not an Indian.

After several decades of contact, however, the Christian dualism of heaven and hell had crept into the beliefs of even those Indians who clung most fervently to tradition. While brave war-

riors and other virtuous Indians still went to the land of the dead, the wicked were sent to wander around a dark land where they were attacked by wild animals. In this way, Christian ideas were absorbed into tribal belief systems even while individual Indians continued to eschew Christianity itself. This process was not new: Indians had always borrowed religious beliefs, deities, and rituals from neighboring groups.

In time this process became more pronounced. A religion expresses a community's understanding of itself as much as of the natural and supernatural worlds. The spread of European civilization across the American continent, which altered the tribes themselves and the natural world around them, naturally altered the tribal religions as well. With the Removal Act of 1830, large eastern tribes like the Cherokee and small ones like the Stockbridge Mahicans were separated from their wooded homelands to live on the windswept Plains or in the wilds of northern Wisconsin—places where their traditional beliefs and rituals, based on the details of daily life, would be senseless. For tribes like the Lakota, the annihilation of the buffalo and their own confinement within reservations rendered many of their old dances, songs, and rituals meaningless. Like the Aztecs' collision with the Spanish, in which the Indians seemed to witness the defeat of their own gods, many North American peoples came to believe that their old way of life, including their spiritual beliefs, had been defeated by a more powerful culture. With their old beliefs no longer valid, some Indians turned to Christianity to help make sense of the new world that had been thrust upon them.

But others refused to relinquish their tribal identity; instead, they reshaped their traditional beliefs in order to come to terms with their oppressive situation, and they sought the help of the powers they had traditionally relied upon whenever they were in physical, social, or spiritual crisis. In some instances, this process developed into new religious movements that gained wide acceptance, and several of these movements were led by men who were received as prophets. These prophets invariably received their sense of purpose and their message in visions induced by illness or deprivation. Often they preached the need for unity among tribes to resist the encroachments of white civilization and

called for a renewal or return to certain traditional beliefs; sometimes, perhaps unconsciously, they incorporated language and imagery of the Christianity that surrounded them.

One of the first of these was the Delaware Prophet, who began preaching in 1762. With his tribe recently displaced from its traditional woodland home in New Jersey and Pennsylvania, a Delaware Indian named Neolin had gone on a spiritual search for the "Master of Life." Finally, one night in a vision, this Great Spirit had given Neolin a stick on which were inscribed his commands: most significantly, to fight no other Indians, to share all food, and to unite all Indians against the white man.

In a similar way, a Shawnee prophet named Lalawethika began preaching in 1805 after falling into a deathlike trance during which he believed he had been taken to the dwelling of the Great Spirit. Lalawethika called on his followers to reject the trappings of white civilization (especially firearms, European-style clothing, and alcohol), and to unite against the whites. After correctly predicting an eclipse, the prophet's popularity grew wildly. He began calling himself *Tenskwatawa*, or "Open Door," and his disciples spread his fame and teachings throughout the East. Under his spiritual leadership and the military leadership of his brother Tecumseh, an intertribal confederation centered at Prophet Town battled the incursion of white settlers into the Ohio Valley. The movement met disaster when Ten-

Tenskwatawa, or Open Door, a Shawnee prophet of the early 1800s. With his powerful and visionary brother Tecumseh, Tenskwatawa called on the eastern tribes to unify and together drive out white settlers.

skwatawa, in his brother's absence, ordered his warriors to attack the troops of William Henry Harrison, telling them they would be protected by his magic. The confederated tribes were badly defeated, thus ending Tecumseh's hopes for an independent Indian nation.

Neither the movement propelled by the Delaware Prophet nor that led by Tenskwatawa could survive, however, as both sought the expulsion or containment of white society, which was militarily more powerful. A more lasting

prophetic movement was founded in 1799, by a Seneca named Handsome Lake.

At the end of the 18th century, the Six Nations of the Iroquois, which included the Seneca, were greatly weakened and demoralized. The six nations had been divided in their allegiances during the American Revolution, some siding with the British while others joined the American colonists and still others remained neutral. After the war, the Iroquois saw their villages burned and lands taken by the victorious American colonies regardless of whom they had supported. Since then, the Seneca as a people had sunk into despair. Handsome Lake himself had been a mighty warrior against the American troops, but by 1799, he too was frequently drunk and seriously ill.

During that summer, as he lay near death, Handsome Lake experienced a vision in which several beings told him that the Creator was unhappy with the state of his people and wanted to make them prosperous and peaceful. The beings then gave Handsome Lake a message and told him to spread it to all the Iroquois. When he emerged from his sickness, Handsome Lake began to preach his code, which came to be known as the *gaiwiio*, or Good Word.

At its core, the religion of Handsome Lake was both Indian and Christian. Although thoroughly Iroquois, Handsome Lake had grown up among Quaker missionaries, three of whom wrote down and helped disseminate the English meaning of his teachings. The

The Spirit of the Corn speaking to Handsome
From a drawing by Jesse Cornplanter,

gaiwiio contained an austere code of discipline that both derived from traditional Iroquois culture and reinforced Quaker teachings. It urged the faithful to give up drinking, dancing, gossip, card playing, adultery, and selling land, because these things were abhorrent to the Great Spirit. In the afterlife, the wicked were condemned to a hell where they were subjected to unending tor-tures. Handsome Lake also taught that a land of the blessed awaited the good Iroquois, a realm that no whites could enter—although a few respected individuals like George Washington were granted a place in a sort of limbo between that domain and hell. As part of his vision for the Iroquois people, Handsome Lake called upon all men to give up war and hunting in order to

, the Seneca prophet
a boy artist

The Seneca prophet Handsome Lake hearing a message from the Corn Spirit. On the verge of death, Handsome Lake had a vision of a time when Indians could live peaceably with whites.

become farmers. Eventually his teachings were collected into a single volume and became known as the "New Religion" of the Iroquois.

Whereas both Tenskwatawa and the Delaware Prophet had in effect looked back to a time that had disappeared with the arrival of Europeans in America, Handsome Lake recognized that white culture was in America to stay. In combining Iroquoian and Christian beliefs, Handsome Lake envisioned a time when the Iroquois could live peacefully as Indians in a white-dominated society.

There were other prophet movements that combined aspects of traditional Indian beliefs with Christianity, but none matched the popularity of the Ghost Dance movement of the late

1800s. The first Ghost Dance movement began in 1870 on the Walker River Reservation of Nevada, when a Northern Paiute Indian named Wodziwob learned in a trance that the dead would soon return to earth and the old tribal life with plentiful game would be restored—if the people faithfully performed certain round dances at night. This Ghost Dance spread quickly through much of California and Oregon among the Paiute, Klamath, Modoc, and Washo tribes. After a few years, the first Ghost Dance died out, in part suppressed by whites and government agents who feared a united Indian uprising, and perhaps quite simply because the dead had not returned as promised by Wodziwob.

In 1889, when tribes in the Great Plains and the West were living on reservations with inadequate supplies and no hope, the second Ghost Dance began. A Northern Paiute Indian named Wovoka (or Jack Wilson), from Mason Valley, Nevada, fell into a trance during an eclipse of the sun. Wovoka's father, Tavibo, had been a disciple of Wodziwob, and probably Wovoka had seen the first Ghost Dance performed. In any event, his message was remarkably similar to Wodziwob's. During his trance, Wovoka was shown the land of the dead:

> When the sun died, I went up to heaven and saw God and all the people who had died a long time ago. God told me to come back and tell my people they must be good and love one another, and

not fight, or steal, or lie. He gave me this dance to give to my people.

A new world was coming, Wovoka was told, and to hasten it he was given a circular dance that his followers must perform for five days in succession. When speaking to whites, Wovoka evidently said that the Ghost Dance would reunite all Indians with their dead loved ones; when speaking to Indians, however, Wovoka proclaimed that the dead, who would be guided by a cloudlike spirit, would return to repeople the land with Indians.

Aided by better transportation and communication, the second Ghost Dance spread rapidly eastward across the Great Plains, where tribes like the Comanche, the Arapaho, the Lakota Sioux, and the Cheyenne were ready to believe anything that would give them hope. The Ghost Dance promised them a renaissance of their old tribal life and the return of their dead; some versions of the message suggested too that whites would be excluded from the new world or indeed driven from it—although Wovoka's own words were clear: "You must not fight. Do no harm to anyone. Do always right." Instead, Wovoka said, there would be a great earthquake, after which only Native Americans would remain on the continent.

Nevertheless, white U.S. officials were alarmed, both by what they took as the message of the religion and by the fact that performances of the Ghost Dance sometimes involved thousands

The visions and words of Wovoka (left) spurred the Ghost Dance movement: "You must not fight. Do no harm to anyone. Do always right." Nevertheless, many white Americans were threatened by the religion. Wovoka is here photographed with an actor, T. J. McCoy, around 1926.

of Indians at a time. On reservations such as those containing various Sioux tribes, officials banned the ceremonies. Many Sioux defied the order, however. Finally, after a series of tense exchanges and misunderstandings, in 1890 U.S soldiers opened fire on a group of Sioux gathered to perform the ceremony at Wounded Knee. More than 300 were killed, most of them women and children. After this tragedy, the second Ghost Dance died quickly, although a few tribes like the Shoshone of Wyoming and Saskatchewan's Lakota still performed it as late as the 1950s.

In many respects, the Ghost Dance religion contained some clearly Christian elements. Wovoka identified—or

(just as important) was believed by his followers to have identified—the cloud-like spirit that would lead the dead home, as Jesus. At times, he taught that Jesus had already returned to earth. "Do not tell the white people about this," Wovoka said in one utterance. "Jesus is now upon the earth. He appears like a cloud. The dead are all alive again. I do not know when they will be here; maybe this fall or in the spring." In addition, both the 1870 and 1890 Ghost Dances had a linear view of history that foresaw a final day of redemption when the dead would come back to life and paradise would be restored. In addition to its parallels to traditional Christian teachings on the Second Coming of Jesus, this apocalyptic view of history contrasted sharply with the cyclical

After the tragedy at Wounded Knee in 1890, performances of the Ghost Dance all but stopped. A scattering of faithful Ghost Dancers remained, though. These Arapaho Indians are shown dancing in 1893.

view of life that was more typical of Indian beliefs. Nevertheless, the Ghost Dance was a religion that rejected white culture—even while adopting some of the precepts of that culture's predominant religion.

Indian prophets thus wove some Christian elements into their traditional beliefs to offer their followers a message of unity and hope in the face of cultural disruption. Some of these prophets, by preaching a message that looked back to a time when their world was devoid of whites, were unable to prepare their followers for the encroaching changes of white society. But a few, like Handsome Lake, offered a vision for the future that included both whites and Indians.

Quanah Parker, a leader of Peyotism. He distinguished between Peyotism and Christianity this way: "The white man goes into his church and talks about Jesus, but the Indian goes into his tipi and talks to Jesus." His deceased mother and baby sister are depicted in the portrait to his right.

"THE SPIRIT OF
THE CIRCLE"

By 1890, the American frontier had vanished. Four centuries after first arriving, white culture had spread across the continent. Missionaries no longer had to proclaim the merits of "civilization" because the Indian tribes no longer had a choice in the matter. They were confined to their reservations, where many attempted to eke out a living as farmers or simply to survive on their tribal annuities. Children were taught mostly in English. Certain Indian customs were outlawed—the Sun Dance, for instance.

Nevertheless, the Indian tribes of the United States and Canada clung to their cultures and languages as expressions of communal identity. One result of this resilient Indian identity was the rise of the Native American Church. This new faith, which first arose in the 1890s among the Indian tribes of the prairies and Great Plains as a peyote cult, combined distinctly Christian and Indian elements and rituals. Like the Ghost Dance religion, it valued altered states of consciousness. But while participants in the Ghost Dance, in its extreme form, longed for the disappearance of all whites from the North American continent, those who followed the peyote cult recognized that the old tribal way of life was permanently lost. In this respect, Peyotism, like the religion of Handsome Lake, tried to preserve central components of Indian spirituality by adopting some aspects of European civilization.

The Aztecs of Mexico had long used the small peyote cactus in their worship. Because of its hallucinogenic qualities—bestowing spiritual visions upon the partaker—the Aztecs viewed the mescaline-containing cactus as "the flesh of the gods." After the Spanish conquest, its sacramental use persisted only in isolated areas, away from the censorious eyes of Spanish priests, who had their own understanding of God's flesh and called peyote "the devil's root." Thus, the peyote cult remained an obscure and persecuted Indian religion in Mexico until the late 19th century, when it spread across the Rio Grande to the Comanche, Kiowa, and Kiowa Apache tribes, and through them, across the Great Plains.

As in Mexico, however, the cult was eyed with suspicion by authorities, who tried to ban the use of peyote. In response, Peyotists in 1918 established a formal church, the Native American Church, to give their religion legal protection.

Unlike the prophet cults, Peyotism had no single figure around whom it coalesced. By some accounts, a half-white, half-Comanche Indian named Quanah Parker was healed from a grave illness by a Mexican Indian medicine woman through the use of peyote. From this woman, Parker learned of the plant's religious and medicinal importance, knowledge that he shared with his Comanche brethren. It was thus at first purely an Indian religion, although like many of the prophet cults, in preaching a pan-Indian spirituality, it also represented a break from the traditional tribal religions.

As the peyote cult spread across the Great Plains, it acquired many Christian traits and eventually evolved into a fusion of Indian tradition and Christianity. There are variations from tribe to tribe, but, according to Emerson Spider, head of the Native American Church in South Dakota, "Because God loves all of us he put this medicine [peyote] in the world so that the Indians would find it and through it they would come to Christ."

Services of the Native American Church usually take place over the course of a Saturday night, beginning at sunset and ending at sunrise. In most tribes, these services are held in specially constructed tipis with doorways facing east, the direction associated with the sacred power of the rising sun. Inside the tipi is an altar that holds traditional ritual paraphernalia, such as eagle and crow feathers, gourd rattles, drums, bowls of water, and plates containing peyote buttons, as well as Christian religious objects such as crosses and Bibles.

Worship is led by a ritualist called the road chief. Over the course of the night, members will eat peyote buttons from a common plate and sing peyote songs, which may consist of standardized verses or of spontaneous lyrics revealed in visions. The songs will be set to a rhythmic beat established by a drum man. Throughout the evening, any number of prayers will be offered, accompanied by smoke from a fire of cedar wood, for the special concerns of the tribe. According to Spider, "During our church services in the tipi we burn the cedar whenever somebody prays, so that the smoke goes up. Our understanding is that we are making smoke signals to the Great Spirit so that He will hear our prayers."

The Native American Church is in many respects a distinctly Indian reli-

Silver and brass peyote pins of the water bird design, made by members of different tribes in Oklahoma and Arizona. Peyote pins often had crescent and star designs as well, symbolizing the altar and the peyote plant, respectively.

gion. Its congregants believe that peyote gives them closer contact with God than that achieved by traditional Christians through prayer alone. Although some individual churches have allowed whites to join and the Church has appealed to some African Americans living near reservations, the Church has remained for the most part a pan-Indian organization. Services are generally conducted in individual tribal languages, unless a congregation includes members of different tribes, in which case English is used. The Church's ritu-als are distinctly Indian, most particularly the use of peyote, which is treated with absolute reverence and seen as a way of lifting the veil between the natural and spiritual realms. For the faithful, in keeping with the traditional understanding of the vision quest, the mind-altering experiences that accompany peyote's use are purely a means of knowing God and God's will for the Indian people.

Despite the uniquely Indian character of the Church's worship, though, its beliefs are just as distinctly Christian.

A peyote drummer. As Peyotism gained popularity among Native Americans, practitioners established the Native American Church in 1918 to avoid government interference.

For instance, for one service Emerson Spider composed four songs in the Lakota language, which in translation read like gospel hymns:

1) I have decided to follow Jesus,
  No turning back.

2) Jesus I love your words
  Because your words are eternal life.
  Give me life.
  I love your words.

3) Praise our Lord Savior Jesus,
  Did you know that our Lord
  Savior Jesus died upon the cross

for our sins?

4) God, look upon us Indians,
  We want to be saved.

Individual interpretations of Native American Church beliefs often blend Christian and Indian images. For instance, one Lakota Sioux described his conversion to Christianity as the result of his peyote-induced vision. He said that he had been leading a "bad" life for many years, and then one night he went to a Native American Church service. During the night, the large peyote button on the altar, sometimes called Chief Peyote, was transformed before his eyes:

> Chief Peyote came out towards me and I saw it. It was a sort of plate that was spinning fast. And in there were classes of people sitting on the plate. The ones that were trying to live according to God's Word were sitting towards the middle. And all those who were not obeying the laws of God were sitting way on the edge of that plate. And I heard people hollering and crying and I saw jails and all other places that did not belong to Christ on the outside of the plate. And I was on the rim of it and I was hanging on and praying that I would live a Christian life . . . and all of a sudden I woke up like and I was sitting on the floor and hanging on to my cushion. This was a vision given to me by Christ through the holy herb.

For this young man, faith in the Native American Church enabled him to reform his life.

The Native American Church has provided a faith to many Indians that has allowed them to retain their cultural identity while coming to terms with a dramatically changed world. Like any religion, it has gone through periods of greater or lesser popularity. Nonetheless, it has spread up the American Great Plains into Saskatchewan and Manitoba, into the Southwest among the Navajo and some branches of the Pueblos, and even among the tribes formerly of the eastern woodlands, now resident both in Oklahoma and around the Great Lakes. At times it has had to endure persecution, both from Christian missionaries, who were suspicious of its nativist elements, and from state and federal authorities, who battled the Church over its use of peyote, a controlled substance. In 1994, however, President William Clinton signed the American Indian Religious Freedom Amendment, finally ensuring the right of the Native American Church to use peyote.

Ultimately, there have been three divergent trends in the Indian reception to and practice of the Christian faith in the 20th century: unconditional acceptance of Christianity, integration of Christian teaching with traditional Indian beliefs, and rejection of Christianity in favor of traditional beliefs.

Many Christian Indians contend that they need to purge their people of all traditional beliefs. According to Francis Hairy Chin, a Lakota deacon of the Roman Catholic Church in South Dakota, "There seems to be too much dwelling on tribal beliefs and old medicine man's practices by most baptized Catholics." On some reservations, independent pentecostal and evangelical churches preach a Bible-based Christianity that calls on the faithful to abandon all traditional beliefs. For example, at the Body of Christ Independent Church, a Pentecostal congregation on the Pine Ridge Reservation in South Dakota, principal minister Eugene Rowland has often preached against the Sun Dance and traditional *yuwipi* (medicine men), calling them "an abomination to God."

Catholic Indians have found special meaning in their devotion to the Blessed Kateri Tekakwitha, who was beatified—named eligible for sainthood—by Pope John Paul II on June 22, 1980. At a mostly Ojibwa congregation in Minneapolis, Mass ends with a prayer in honor of the Blessed Kateri, whom many hope and pray the Church will soon canonize as its first North American Indian saint. According to Francis Hairy Chin, being a Christian Indian means acquiring "the faith spirit of the Kateri Tekakwitha." Each year the National Tekakwitha Catholic Conference draws over two thousand delegates, and thousands of Catholic Indians make a pilgrimage to the Caughnawaga Indian Reservation in Quebec, where she is buried, and to Auriesville, New York, where she was born. In this respect, the Blessed Kateri Tekakwitha meets the same need for many Catholic Native Americans as Our Lady of Guadalupe did for the Catholic Indians of Mexico—a sense that God extended his favor and protection to them as a people.

The growth and popularity of the Native American Church typifies the second of these trends—an increasing tendency to blend Indian traditions with Christian beliefs and worship. In addition to the Native American Church, this trend has taken two forms. First, many denominations that have long ministered to the reservations and to the growing population of urban Indians have begun to incorporate traditional Indian rituals, symbols, and prayers into their services of Christian

worship. For instance, Catholic Indians at the Congregation of the Great Spirit in Milwaukee celebrate Mass each week with cedar and sage smoke wafting through the air; prayers are offered to God in both English and Potawatomi and then "put" on strands of tobacco and burned in a fire in front of the altar. In a similar vein, Sunday school students at the Episcopal Church of the Holy Comforter on the Lower Brule Sioux Reservation in South Dakota use a curriculum entitled "In the Spirit of the Circle." One lesson features White Buffalo Calf Woman, who is compared to John the Baptist; just as she prepared her people to receive the sacred pipe, says the lesson, so John the Baptist prepared the people of Israel to receive the coming of Christ.

In addition, many Indians now feel comfortable practicing both some form of Christianity and a traditional Indian spirituality. Ed Red Eagle of the Osage tribe is a devout Catholic and a leader in his tribe's services in the Native American Church, and he claims that both religions teach "a faith in the same Almighty God." In a similar way, some Lakota participate in their tribe's traditional Sun Dance while remaining faithful members of various Christian denominations on their reservations. Moreover, among some tribes, the Sun Dance has been reinterpreted to fit with Christian theology: some members of the Shoshone, for instance, pray to Jesus during the Sun Dance and compare the Sun Dance lodge to the grave of Christ, through which one must pass to find

Five Arizona Hopis visit with Bishop Phillip G. Sher, who once instructed them in Christian doctrine. The occasion for the visit was the Serra Festival, honoring Junipero Serra, at Carmel Mission.

eternal life—concepts they have picked up from attendance at Catholic, Episcopal, and Mormon mission churches.

For many Indians, however, the Christian and Indian spiritual traditions are incompatible and should not be blended. A third trend has thus been a rejection of Christianity as destructive of Indian ways of life. In keeping with this rejection, some Indians have advocated a return to a traditional Indian spirituality. For instance, Vine Deloria, Jr., a Lakota and the son and grandson of Episcopal priests, has stated in his book *God Is Red* that most of the problems facing Indians as individuals and tribes—and American society as a whole—stem from a warped view of humanity and the world preached by Christianity: "Where did Westerners get their ideas of divine right to conquest, of manifest destiny, of themselves as the vanguard of true civilization, if not from Christianity?"

The divisions among Native Americans' acceptance of Christianity reflect the history of forced change that began in the 15th century with the arrival of the first Europeans. Some Native Americans, like Thomas Mayhew's Wampanoag protégé Hiacoomes, adopted Christianity quickly and sincerely; others, like Sitting Bull, were eloquent in defending their own beliefs. Most Native Americans fell somewhere in between these poles. Whether they secretly worshipped their own spirits while ostensibly accepting Catholicism (like the Mexica people after Cortés's conquest), or observed Russian Orthodox rituals faithfully but with little understanding (like the Aleuts of the

Sacred Heart Catholic Church became a military bunker when American Indian Movement activists took over Wounded Knee, South Dakota, in 1973. The seizure of the town and occupation of the church was a militant response to a long history of forced acculturation.

early 19th century), Native Americans rarely embraced European religions without resisting.

Contrary to European stereotypes of Native Americans as "savages" or as empty vessels waiting to be filled with the word of a Christian God, America's first inhabitants had vital and vibrant religions that explained their surroundings and sustained their hopes. Ultimately, Native Americans selected the elements of Christianity that offered meaning in a radically changed world, while preserving the elements of their traditional beliefs to keep their Indian identity alive for future generations.

BIBLIOGRAPHY

Bonvillain, Nancy. *Native American Religion*. New York: Chelsea House Publishers, 1996.

Coleman, Michael C. *Presbyterian Missionary Attitudes Toward American Indians, 1837-1893*. Jackson: University Press of Mississippi, 1985.

Deloria, Vine, Jr. Vine *God Is Red: A Native View of Religion*. 2nd ed. Golden, Colorado: North American Press, 1992.

DeMallie, Raymond J., and Douglas R. Parks, eds. *Sioux Indian Religion: Tradition and Innovation*. Norman: University of Oklahoma Press, 1987.

Hultkrantz, Ake. *Belief and Worship in Native North America*. Syracuse: Syracuse University Press, 1981.

Jennings, Francis. *The Invasion of America: Indians, Colonialism, and the Cant of Conquest*. Chapel Hill: The University of North Carolina Press, 1975.

McLoughlin, William G. *Cherokees and Missionaries, 1789-1839*. New Haven: Yale University Press, 1984.

Noley, Homer. *First White Frost: Native Americans and United Methodism*. Nashville: Abingdon Press, 1991.

Rivera, Luis N. *A Violent Evangelism*. Louisville: Westminster/John Knox Press, 1991.

Szasz, Margaret Connell. *Indian Education in the American Colonies, 1607-1783*. Albuquerque: University of New Mexico Press, 1988.

Tinker, George E. *Missionary Conquest: The Gospel and Native American Cultural Genocide*. Minneapolis: Augsburg Fortress, 1993.

Trent, James, ed. *Native and Christian: Indigenous Voices on Religious Identity in the United States and Canada*. New York: Routledge, 1995.

GLOSSARY

apostatize To renounce one's religious faith.

benevolent With good will; disposed to do good.

canonize To officially recognize a deceased person as a saint.

encomiendo System in which encomenderos—Spanish soldiers who had been allotted land and Indian workers—supervised the forced labor of their people.

fiefdom Territory over which one has control.

gaiwiio Seneca term for the "Good Word" as preached by Handsome Lake.

hierarchical Strictly arranged by rank or class.

Kiehtan The Wampanoag creator.

longhouse A long, communal dwelling made of wood, built by the Iroquoian tribes.

ononharoia Literally, "turning the brain upside down." An annual ceremony observed by the Huron, during which people tried to fulfill each other's secret desires through dream interpretation.

pantheon All of the recognized gods of a people.

pantribal Involving the union of all Native American tribes.

powwaws Wampanoag healers who supervised religious ceremonies.

presidio A fortified settlement in an area under Spanish control.

promyshlenniki Russian trappers and traders who settled on the Northern Pacific Coast in the 18th century.

road chief Ritualist in the Native American Church who organizes worship services and supplies peyote.

sachem A North American Indian chief.

shaman A priest who uses magic to heal the sick, predict the future, and control events.

taboo A prohibition or restriction observed to ensure protection against supernatural harm.

wakan A general term for spirit power, originating with the Great Plains tribes.

INDEX

STEVE KLOTS, a native of Tennessee, holds a bachelor of arts degree from Trinity College in Connecticut and a master of divinity degree from Harvard University. He has also done postgraduate work studying the role of religion in society at Otago University in Dunedin, New Zealand. The author of three other Chelsea House books (*Richard Allen, Ida Wells-Barnett,* and *Carl Lewis*), he is chaplain of South Kent School in Connecticut.

FRANK W. PORTER III, general editor of INDIANS OF NORTH AMERICA, is director of the Chelsea House Foundation for American Indian Studies. He holds a B.A., M.A., and Ph.D. from the University of Maryland. He has done extensive research concerning the Indians of Maryland and Delaware and is the author of numerous articles on their history, archaeology, geography, and ethnography. He was formerly director of the Maryland Commission on Indian Affairs and American Indian Research and Resource Institute, Gettysburg, Pennsylvania, and he has received grants from the Delaware Humanities Forum, the Maryland Committee for the Humanities, the Ford Foundation, and the National Endowment for the Humanities, among others. Dr. Porter is the author of *The Bureau of Indian Affairs* in the Chelsea House KNOW YOUR GOVERNMENT series.

PICTURE CREDITS

2:	map illustration by Sandra L. Taccone	47:	The Bettmann Archive
12:	American Museum of Natural History	49:	UPI/Bettmann
		50:	Special Collections Division, University of Washington Libraries
15:	The Bettmann Archive		
16:	University of Utah Press, Salt Lake City	53:	American Museum of Natural History
19:	The Bettmann Archive	54:	Library of Congress
20-21:	American Museum of Natural History	57:	Library of Congress
		58-59:	Santa Barbara Mission Archives
23:	Library of Congress		
24:	The Whaling Museum, New Bedford, Massachusetts	60:	Woolaroc Museum
		63:	Library of Congress
27:	The Bettmann Archive	64:	Harvard University, Houghton Library
28:	The Bettmann Archive		
31:	The Bettmann Archive	67:	Woolaroc Museum
32:	The Bettmann Archive	68:	Walters Art Gallery, Baltimore
35:	American Museum of Natural History	71:	American Museum of Natural History
36:	Library of Congress	72-73:	American Museum of Natural History
38:	National Archives of Canada, #6643	75:	American Museum of Natural History
41:	McCord Museum of Canadian History, Montreal	76-77:	Nebraska State Historical Society
42:	Library of Congress	79:	Latter Day Saints Church Archives, Salt Lake City, Utah
45:	National Archives of Canada, #71502		
46:	National Archives of Canada, #1470	80:	South Dakota State Historical

	Society		
83:	The Newberry Library		
84-85:	Library of Congress		
87:	Smithsonian Institution		
88-89:	Smithsonian Institution		
90:	Smithsonian Institution		
93:	Museum of the American Indian, Heye Foundation		
94:	Philadelphia Museum of Art: purchased with funds from the American Museum of Photography		
97:	The Bettmann Archive		
98-99:	UPI/Bettmann		

color section:

photo #1, #2, #3:	South Dakota Art Museum Collection, Brookings, South Dakota
photo #4:	Buddy Mays/TRAVEL STOCK
photo #5	FPG International
photo #6:	Photo Researchers, Inc.
photo #7:	Photo Researchers, Inc., photo by Vanessa Vick
photo #8:	Courtesy of the Fonda National Shrine of Blessed Kateri Tekakwitha, Fonda, NY